Model Railroa

Rutger Friberg

**Published by
Allt om Hobby**

Model Railroad Electronics 1
Second revised edition

Author: Rutger Friberg

Original title: Elektronik för modelljärnvägen
English translation: Joel Ernest

Cover photo: Jens Dahlström
Other photos by the author, Jens Dahlström or from the *Allt om Hobby* archives

Layout: Peter Liander and Mattias Stenbom

The series Model Railroad Electronics, by
Rutger Friberg, also includes the following titles:
Model Railroad Electronics 2, 1995, ISBN 91-85496-82-0
Model Railroad Electronics 3, 1996, ISBN 91-85496-91-X
Model Railroad Electronics 4, 1997, ISBN 91-85496-51-0
Model Railroad Electronics 5, 1997, ISBN 91-85496-52-9

ISBN 91-85496-96-0
First published in the English language in 1994. First edition ISBN 91-85496-73-1

Publisher: Allt om Hobby AB, Box 90 133, S-120 21 Stockholm, Sweden.
Fax +46-8-99 88 66, E-mail: freddy.stenbom@hobby.se

Printed in Sweden by Gummessons Tryckeri AB, Falköping 1997

Foreword

This book was first published in Sweden in 1986. As a publisher I was afraid that the subject was too narrow for the Swedish model railroaders but I decided anyway that we should give the book a chance. I am glad that I was totally wrong at that time, the book was the answer to many questions and it was also on the right level for all modelers who – without any knowledge in electronics – would like to give it a try.

This book proved to be the "Cookbook" for all beginners and also for more experienced railroaders. Everybody could find something that would improve their present layout and also a lot of ideas for future planning. On the following pages the readers will find more than 30 electronic projects as well as various "miniguides" – construction ideas, component descriptions and instructional material. You may call it an "Encyclopedia of model railroad electronics".

This is the second edition of this book in English. We have revised, updated and improved the book's contents. We have used color to improve some of the schematics and explanatory illustrations. This work was done by my son Mattias who actually was involved with the Swedish edition (at age 8) in 1986.

The Author Rutger Friberg was born in Stockholm, Sweden in 1945 and has been a railroader since childhood. He is now living in Gothenburg and working as a director at corporate level at Volvo. Among other things, he is looking at new technologies and in his spare time he tries out – plays with if you like – new materials in his hobby long before others have a chance to do the same.

Rutger Friberg emphasizes that model railroading has many facets, from the pure artistic viewpoint to model design and advanced electronics. With his background in electronic engineering it is not surprising that he has specialized in the electronic aspects of this hobby. Rutger is now being recognized in many parts of the railroading world, he is working independently with the international model railroad industry, both as an adviser and product developer. For the US audience he might be best known for his well received workshops and clinics at the NMRA National Conventions and his close connection with the NMRA-DCC committee.

Rutger Friberg has written a number of articles in the Swedish magazine Allt om Hobby for more than 15 years. He has also published five books and is currently working on a sixth one in the same series with more technical ideas for railroaders. The other books have already been published in English and the sixth will be out to the US market during the following year.

Rutger has other interests besides model railroading. A well filled trophy cabinet testifies to his past achievements as an amateur power boat and auto racer. He has also been the navigator on large offshore sailing boat races. He says that model railroading is a hobby that is at its best when accepted by the entire family. He likes to point out that the understanding of his wife, Susanne, and his two children, Oscar and Sofia, made it possible for him to find the time to experiment, design and test the many projects in this book.

Freddy Stenbom,
Publisher, Allt om Hobby AB

Introduction

This book has been fun to write and I hope you'll enjoy it.

You won't need a degree in electrical engineering to use this book. Most of the tips and projects are suitable for beginners. It's not absolutely necessary to understand the function of each and every component but if you can learn a little from each completed project it'll pay off when you start designing your own circuits. For this reason, I've mixed in a little theory with practice.

If you, dear reader, are among the curious that haven't yet entered the hobby of model-railroading I hope that this book will lead you a bit on the way towards a very educational, relaxing and interesting hobby.

Rutger Friberg

Tools

This chapter is primarily directed towards the novist electronics hobbyist. We'll be taking a look at the tools you'll be using, some shopping tips, basic techniques and a few important words on safety.

Most homes have at least a few basic tools about - a hammer, a screwdriver or two, a pair of pliers and maybe a saw of some sort. Nothing against these tools, but for electronics work, they are completely inadequate.

While the projects in this book vary in degree of difficulty from the very simple to the more complicated, they all have a common ground in modern electronics. Consequently, the components are small and make little demand on space. You'll need tools and instruments designed for working in tight quarters.

I've made a list of the items you'll need to get started. For a rather low cash outlay you'll be able to construct and test any or all of the projects in this book. You can expect to pay in the neighborhood of 60 to 70 dollars to put together this basic kit.

A relatively expensive item on the list is the battery powered drill. Even if you already own a standard, household drill I think you'll find that the smaller and lighter battery powered models are well worth their price. Besides the fact that standard drills seldom accept the smaller sizes of drillbits often used in electronics construction, you'll avoid the irritation of a power cord that always seems to be in the way. The drill kit often includes a set of bits. Buy extras. They do wear out and breakage is common. If you don't have all that steady a hand, consider buying a drillmotor stand.

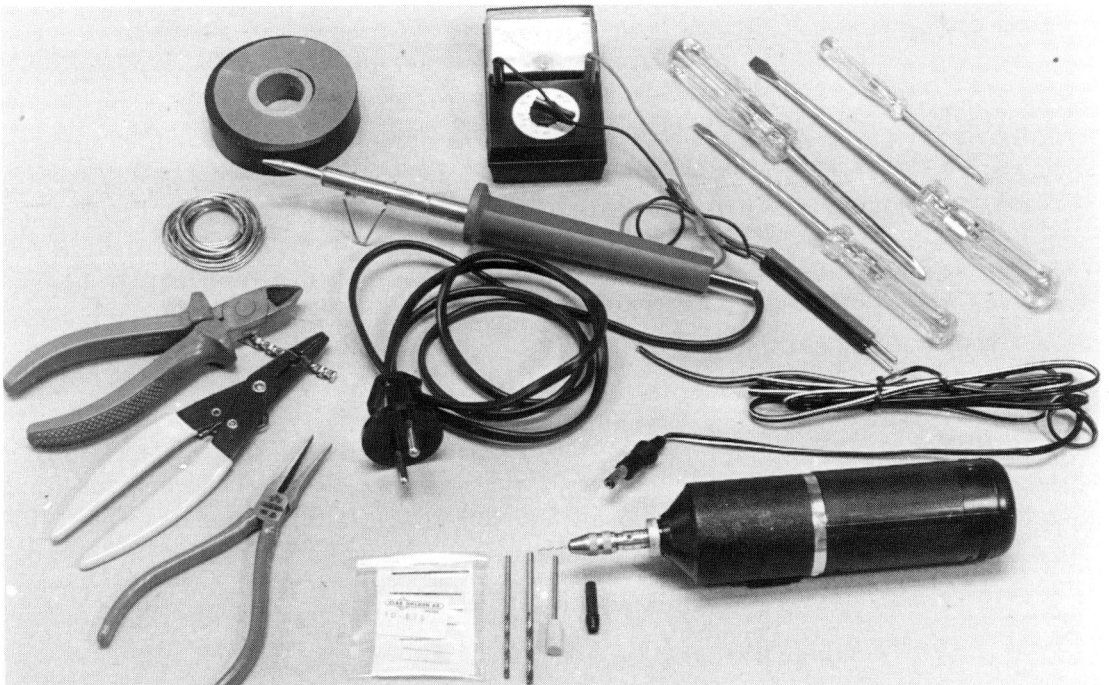

The basic tool kit for electronics construction: multitester, screwdriver set, soldering iron, solder, drill motor, drills, wire cutters, long nose pliers, wire strippers and electrical tape.

The soldering iron should be between 25 and 30 watts. Avoid the common, hardware store variety. They produce too much heat and are awkward to use because of their large tips. Size also rules out soldering guns. If you can afford it, a soldering station is by far the best choice.

Your choice of solder is critical. Use only rosin core solder. Acid core corrodes electrical connections and components.

Wirestrippers can be purchased for under five dollars but good ones can cost four times as much. Generally, the price of a tool is a good indicator of its quality.

INSTRUMENTS

Just as important as having the right tools is access to test instruments. Troubleshooting would be almost impossible without some form of test instrument.

Some of the projects in this book deal with the construction of test instruments but even those circuits may require testing and the correction of construction errors. Experience has shown that at least one construction error seems to find its way into each project. Therefore, I suggest investing in a small multitester.

Multitesters measure voltage, amperage and resistance. You'll need one able to measure up to 250 volts. The capacity to measure milliamperes is also necessary. The better instruments give readings for both direct and alternating current. A top-end current measuring range of up to five to ten amps is desirable.

SOLDERING

This isn't going to be a course in soldering but rather, due to space limitations, a collection of tips. Keep in mind that a soldering iron is a hot tool. You'll burn yourself if you come in contact with the tip. Develop the habit of ALWAYS pulling out the plug as soon as you've finished soldering. Leaving a hot iron unattended is asking for trouble.

Soldering iron stands are inexpensive and reduce the risk of fire considerably. Enough said!

You won't learn to solder overnight. This is a case of practice makes perfect and I recommend practising on something cheap. The trick is to solder "just enough". Beginners often "cold solder" – using too little heat before applying the solder. On the other hand, too much heat will damage electrical components. "Just enough" is when the iron is held at the connection to be soldered for a second or so before touching the solder to the joint. Continue until the solder has spread out evenly and no longer resembles a clump-like, metal pearl. This usually takes an additional second or two.

The longer the wire to be soldered, the longer it takes to heat the solder to its melting temperature. Soldering a small component to a larger can be tricky. It's easy to overheat the smaller component. Taking a grip with a pair of needle nose pliers between the component and the soldering point will draw off much of the heat. The pliers function as a heat sink.

As you solder, slag will form on the iron's tip. Between soldering sessions the tip will usually oxidize. Do not clean the iron with a file. I use a small damp sponge for cleaning and it's always close at hand. Before each soldering operation I wipe the tip across the sponge. It'll give off a little steam but leaves the tip nice and clean.

SAFETY

The only life threatening risk with electronics work is coming in contact with 120 volt alternating current. Because of this I have refrained from including projects involving high voltage circuits. The low currents and voltages found on the electronic modules themselves pose no safety hazards. When it comes to powering the modules, use Underwriters approved transformers.

GENERAL

Always work carefully and never try to rush through a project. It's easy to connect a diode or electrolytic capacitor backwards. Check and double check.

Both Radio Shack and Jameco are good sources for tools and components. With Radio Shack's 7,000 outlets, you probably have a store within driving range. Jameco offers mail order service. Their address is 1355 Shoreway Road, Belmont, California 94002. From 7 AM to 4 PM PST you can reach them at (415) 592-8097.

Finally, a few words on static electricity. That's the phenomenon that occurs when you walk across a wall to wall carpet and then touch the refrigerator door. You get a shock! What happens is that the body is charged by the carpet. Contact with the refrigerator releases the charge. If you had touched an electronic component, the charge would have passed to the component. CMOS integrated circuits are especially sensitive for static electricity discharges. For this reason, avoid working in rooms with wall to wall carpeting.

	USA (Radio Shack)	UK (Maplin)
Minidrill*	MS 398	1 BW03D
Drill bit set*	22PDK	1 LH78K
Diagonal cutter	64-1930	1 JH27E
Screwdriver kit	64-1948	1 BR58N
8-22 gauge stripper	64-1919	1 BR76H
Long-Nose Pliers	64-1844	1 BR77J
5-piece soldering tools	64-2802	1 FY68Y
Rosin Core solder	64-001	1 FV53H
Multitester	22-215	1 YJ76H
Electrical tape	64-2340	1 FT24B

* Jameco

For UK readers:

Maplin (Shops in 12 cities)
P.O. Box 3
Rayleigh
Essex, SS6 8LR
0702-554161
0702-553935 fax

Cirkit
53 Burrfieldes Road
Portsmouth
Hants, PO3 5EB
0705-669021
0705-695485 fax

Greenweld Electronics Ltd
27 Park Road
Southampton
SO1 3TB
0703-236363
0703-236307 fax

Blinking lights

On a model railroad, we're always looking for ways to liven up the layout. Naturally, the trains themselves headline the show but lighting can also do much to enhance the overall effect. In this chapter we'll be constructing a blinking light chain.

Each miniature light bulb on a model railroad consumes 50 to 100 mA (milli-amps), depending on the amount of light it puts out. The AC outputs on most transformers commonly deliver a maximum of one amp (1000 mA =1 A). In that both switches and lighting share that same AC output, the number of bulbs that can be connected to one transformer is rather limited.

Miniature light bulbs have a relatively short life span. They are also expensive. A better and less expensive alternative is the LED (light emitting diode). Although they usually need to be connected to current reducing resistors they are far superior to bulbs in applications requiring points of light (for example, railroad and highway signals, road construction warning lights, advertising signs, etc.). Besides having an extremely long life span, they are also manufactured in both blinking and non-blinking versions.

We'll be using both versions to construct this blinking light circuit. Besides the LEDs, the only other component required is a small resistor. The circuit is designed for a 12 to 16 volt DC power source. If you are using your AC output as a power source, rectify the AC to DC by bridging the plus and minus wires shown on the drawing with a standard diode. The circuit can also be powered by batteries. The LEDs will blink at a frequency of 1 to 2 Hz (Hertz) which means that they will blink one or two times per second.

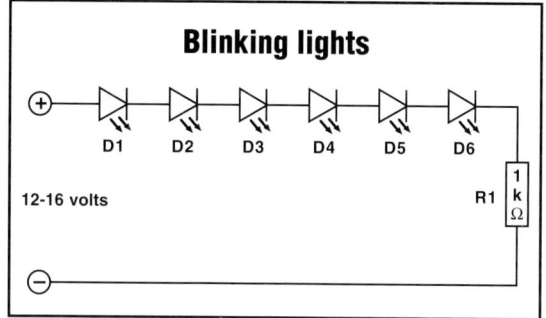

Blinking lights

LEDs can be purchased in both five millimeter and three millimeter versions. The standard 5 mm LED is cheaper. The smaller LEDs can cost up to twice as much as the larger ones.

CONSTRUCTION

As shown on the drawing, we'll be connecting all of the components in series (in a chain, one after the other). Although the resistor will work regardless of which leg is connected to plus or minus, the LEDs must be connected correctly to operate. The symbol for a diode is an arrowhead with a cross line at its tip. The cross line represents the diode's cathode and must be connected to minus. The cathodes on LEDs are mar-

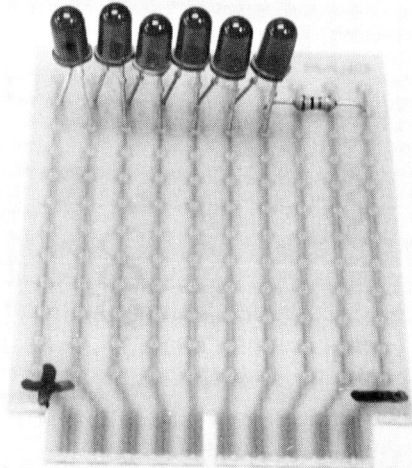

ked by a flat spot on the plastic portion of the LED. The leg closest to the flat spot is the cathode. Often the cathode legs are shorter than the longer anode legs. Only one of the LEDs in this circuit is a blinking LED. It doesn't matter where in the chain it is connected. You'll be able to identify the blinking version by its very short third leg. While this third leg is not to be connected, it is necessary for the diode's blinking function.

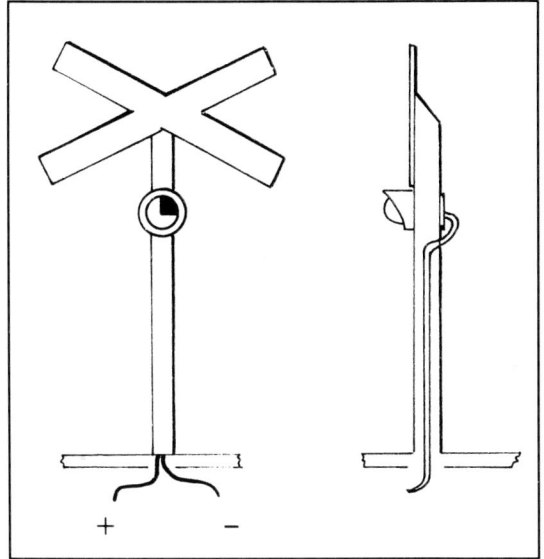

CONNECTIONS

You'll notice immediately if you connect this circuit improperly to your power source - it won't work! As you have probably realized, it isn't necessary to mount the LEDs on the circuit board. Place them on the layout as required and connect them to the circuit board with thin wire. As long as they are still connected in series, you won't have any problems. You can increase the amount of diodes by two if your power source is in the 15 to 18 volt range.

Components	USA	UK
1 LED - blinking red	276-036	1 QY98G
1 kit (20 LEDs)	276-1622	5 UK48C
1 resistor 1kΩ/0.25W	271-1321	1 M1K
1 experimental perfboard	276-1395	1 JP47B
1 card-edge-connector	276-1564	1 FL86T

Miniguide
Resistor Color Code

Stripe number

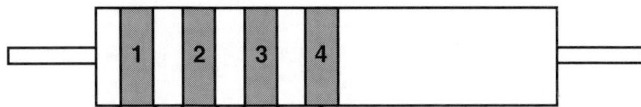

Example		Stripe 1	Stripe 2	Multiplier	Tolerance
3 red stripes	Black	0	0	x 1 Ω	Silver = 10 %
= 2,000 ohm	Brown	1	1	x 10 Ω	Gold = 5 %
= 2.2 kilo ohm	Red	2	2	x 100 Ω	
= 2.2 K	Orange	3	3	x 1,000 Ω	
	Yellow	4	4	x 10,000 Ω	
	Green	5	5	x 100,000 Ω	
	Blue	6	6	x 1,000,000 Ω	
	Violet	7	7	x 10,000,000 Ω	
	Gray	8	8	x 100,000,000 Ω	
	White	9	9	x 1,000,000,000 Ω	

Voltage regulator

You'll sometimes need to regulate voltages. Your power source may be a battery pack or a transformer with an output of 18 volts. If you want to power an accessory that requires a voltage of 12 volts you'll need a voltage regulator. In this chapter we'll be building a regulator with a variable voltage output.

Our voltage regulator consists of just five components. It is both inexpensive and simple to build. It can be powered by up to 24 volts DC. It's output varies from just above zero to nearly its input voltage. As long as your power needs are less than 300mA, you won't need a heat sink for the transistor.

The 2N3055 is a power transistor than can handle currents of up to 15A. The more current that the transistor is required to regulate, the warmer it'll become. The heat can be disappated by mounting the transistor on a heat sink. Larger current flows demand larger heat sinks. Ready-made heat sinks are available with pre-drilled holes. Power transistors are often cooled by mounting them on metal accessory enclosures. A simple rule of thumb for transistor cooling is that if the transistor is too warm to touch, cooling is insufficient.

In most cases, setting your output voltage is a one time affair. If you do plan to use it in an application requiring a variable voltage (such as powering a small motor), equip the potentiometer with a knob.

CONSTRUCTION
If you aren't familiar with the components used in this project see the section on component descriptions, towards the end of the book. Begin construction by placing the

components on the circuit board to check that you'll have room for everything.

The photo shows my prototype for this project. I included a twelve volt lightbulb. Circuit boards can be altered by cutting through the copper strips but you can avoid the extra work through careful, component layout planning.

On my prototype I chose to first solder the transistor's two legs to the circuit board. Via a soldering tab (a common flat washer will suffice) and a short piece of wire, I connected the transistor's metal case (the collector) to the regulator's plus input terminal. One tab of the potentiometer was also connected at this point. The zener diode was then attached between the transistor's base and the regulator's minus terminal. Another of the potentiometer's tabs was

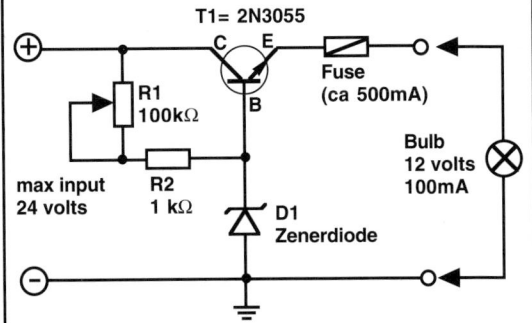

Voltage regulator

T1= 2N3055

max input
24 volts

R1
100kΩ

R2
1 kΩ

Fuse
(ca 500mA)

Bulb
12 volts
100mA

D1
Zenerdiode

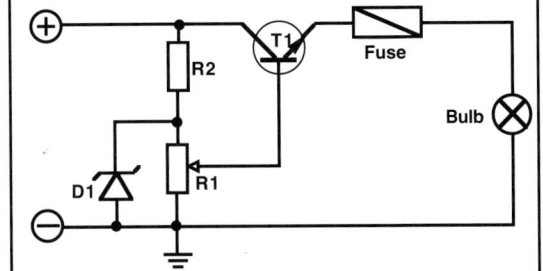

Alternate circuit

R2

T1

Fuse

Bulb

D1

R1

connected to the base via a 1 kΩ resistor. Finally, the transistor's emitter was connected to the plus output terminal.

As designed, this regulator's maximum output is restrained to 12 volts. To raise or lower the maximum voltage, substitute the circuit's 12 to 13 volt zener diode for one of a higher or lower value.

The regulator works as both a voltage and current limiter. Compared with a fuse that self destructs at high current flow, the regulator limits the flow. But don't think of it as an electronic fuse. It's reaction time is too slow.

CONNECTIONS

Connecting the voltage regulator to the layout is simple in that only three wires need be connected. First connect the common minus (or ground). Follow up by connecting the plus in and output terminals.

Components	USA	UK
1 transistor 2N3055	276-2041	1 YH98G
1 experimental perfboard	276-1395	1 JP47B
1 linear potentiometer100KΩ	271-092	1 FW05F
1 zener diode 12 volts/0.4W*	276-563	1 QH16S
1 bulb 12V - 100mA	272-1127	1 WL80B
1 bulb adapter	272-357	1 RX86T
1 card-edge-connector	276-1564	1 FL86T
		* Jameco

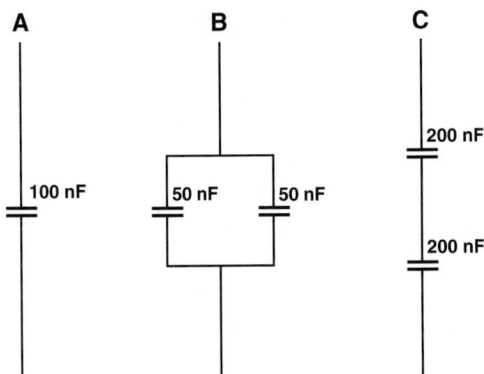

Miniguide

A   B   C

100 nF   50 nF   50 nF

200 nF

200 nF

A = B = C = 100 nF

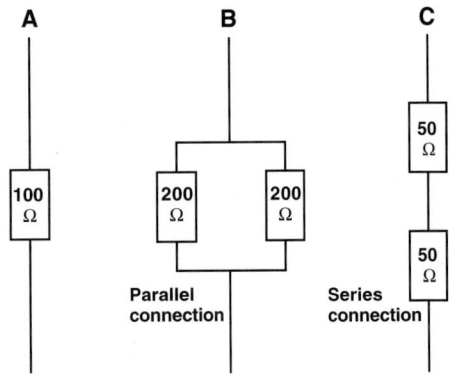

Miniguide

A   B   C

100 Ω

200 Ω   200 Ω

50 Ω

50 Ω

Parallel connection

Series connection

A = B = C = 100 Ω

Current limiter

Both light bulbs and LEDs have the disadvantage of light levels that rise and fall in proportion to changing currents and voltages. Let's take the headlight of a model locomotive as an example. The faster the locomotive is run, the brighter the headlight shines. A current limiter will cure this problem. You'll get a stable beam of light regardless of how much the voltage varies within the three to 25 volt range.

This project uses just six active components. It's both inexpensive and easy to build. Being a staunch supporter of LEDs, I have replaced the loco's headlight bulb with a LED.

CONSTRUCTION

For demonstration purposes I have assembled the circuit on a somewhat oversized circuit board. Two resistors, two NPN signal transistors, a diode and a LED are the only components required for the basic circuit. As you can see in the photo, the components take little space. They would easily fit on a smaller circuit board for mounting in most model locomotive shells. Take note of how the transistors are connected to each other. If you aren't sure of which legs are which, turn to the section on component descriptions.

This circuit can be used in any situation where a constant level of light is desireable. If you plan to use it on a locomotive, please take note of the following. As shown, the headlight will only light in one direction of travel. If you want the headlight to shine regardless of direction of travel, substitute D1 for a small bridge rectifier. For locomotives with headlights at both ends, omit D1 and construct two current limiting circuits. Wire the two so that the plus of one is the minus of the other. The headlights will now be directional.

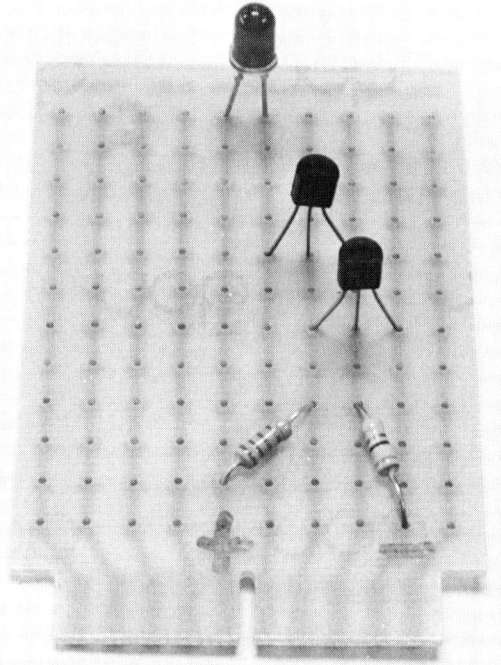

If space is limited under the locomotive shell omit the circuit board and solder the components directly to each other. For a more prototypical appearance, the plastic tip of a LED can be slightly flattened with a file or sandpaper. If you go this route, buy a few extra LEDs. Too much filing will destroy a LED.

If either of the transistors or diodes are improperly connected the circuit will not function. An excellent way of testing the circuit is to connect it to a battery pack. 3 to 4.5 volts is appropriate for this project. If you have made a faulty connection, the battery voltage will not harm the components.

Current regulator

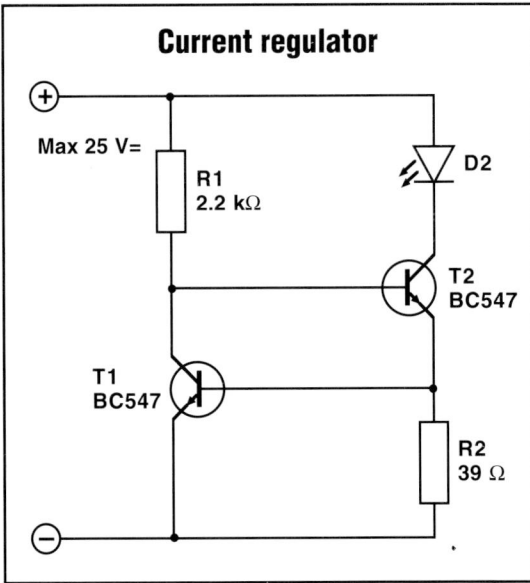

(+) Max 25 V=

R1
2.2 kΩ

D2

T2
BC547

T1
BC547

R2
39 Ω

(−)

CONNECTIONS

Plus is normally the right hand rail in the direction of travel. Connect the circuit's plus terminal to the motor terminal wired to the right hand rail pickup. Note that some locomotives are wired with the plus on the left. If you discover that you have "lefty locos", there is no need to convert them. Just connect the current limiter's plus terminal to the left side of the locomotive instead.

Components	USA	UK
1 LED 5 mm red	276-044	1 UK48C
2 transistors BC 547	276-2009	2 QQ14Q
1 resistor 2.2 kΩ/0.25W	271-1325	1 M2.2K
1 resistor 39 Ω/0.25W*	271-312	1 M39R
1 experimental Perfboard	276-1395	1 JP47B
1 card-edge-connector	276-1564	1 FL86T
* available only in assortment set of 500 pieces		

Light dimmer

In this chapter we'll be building a simple light dimmer. You'll be able to connect up to 20 miniature light bulbs to this circuit.

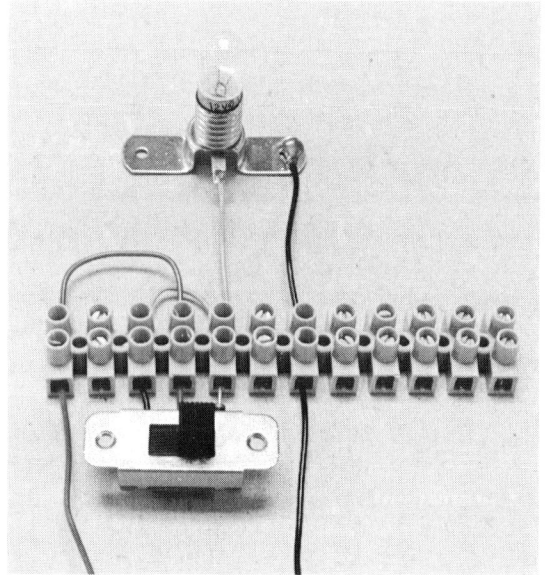

We'll be taking advantage of one of the common diode's most important characteristics. Namely, that when a diode is connected into a circuit it creates a voltage drop of .6 volts.

A practical application of the diode's voltage dropping characteristic can be utilized in reducing a power source's output to match the load. If we had a power source of three volts and needed to power a 1.8 volt light bulb we could connect two diodes in series (one after the other) between the power source and the bulb. In that each diode would drop the output voltage by .6 volts, the combined drop would be 1.2 volts, leaving 1.8 volts to power the lamp.

A diode only passes current in one direction- the diode's "forward". If a diode is connected "backwards" it blocks the current flow.

Connect as many diodes as required in your own circuit to attain the desired voltage level. The diode or diodes can handle up to one amp. That's a load of about 20 miniature light bulbs.

CONSTRUCTION

There is no need to use a circuit board for this project. You can solder the diodes directly to the switch, at the load itself or anywhere in between.

The schematic shows a simple version of

Miniguide

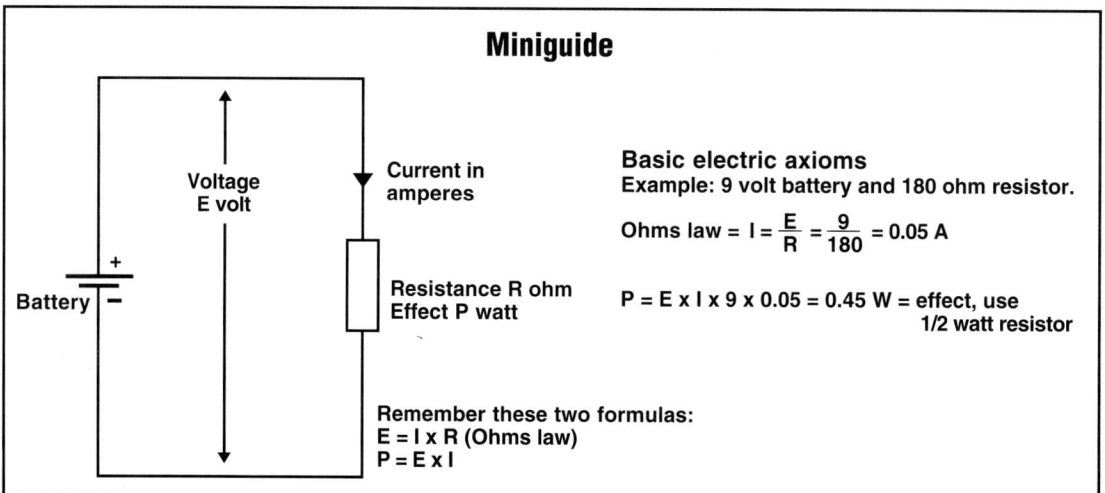

Voltage
E volt

Current in amperes

Resistance R ohm
Effect P watt

Battery

Basic electric axioms
Example: 9 volt battery and 180 ohm resistor.

Ohms law = $I = \dfrac{E}{R} = \dfrac{9}{180} = 0.05\ A$

$P = E \times I \times 9 \times 0.05 = 0.45\ W$ = effect, use
1/2 watt resistor

Remember these two formulas:
E = I x R (Ohms law)
P = E x I

the dimmer switch. Use a multi-step switch with varying amounts of diodes at each step to gradually decrease the output voltage to your lamps or to reduce an accessory's motor speed. For some applications, a relay may be more suitable than a switch. The relay could be controlled by your trains via trackmounted reed switches.

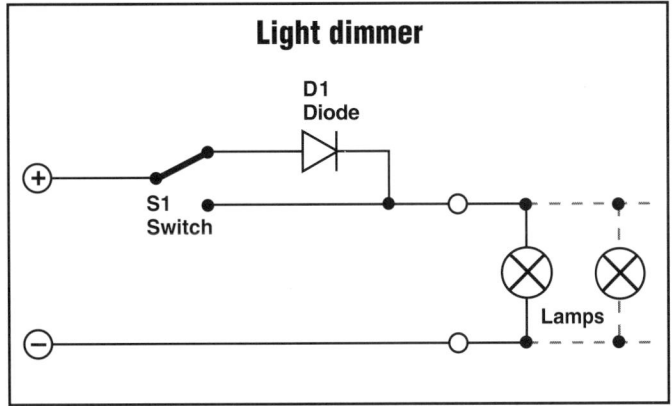

Light dimmer

Components	USA	UK
1 diode 1N4001	276-1101	1 QL73Q
1 slide switch SPDT	275-409	1 FF77J
1 12-way terminal block	274-679	1 FE78K
1 bulb 12V-100mA	272-1127	1 WL80B
1 bulb adapter	272-357	1 RX86T

Test probe

Model railroads have a tendency to become electrical snakepits. Connection errors and sudden, unexplainable short circuits are common. The only chance of attaining a high level of operational reliability is through orderliness and documentation.

Unfortunately, despite your best efforts, electrical problems can arise. The simple test probe described in this chapter will indicate both voltage and polarity.

Just as the name light emitting diode implies, a LED is a diode that lights. As in the common diodes, a LED also reduces a circuit's voltage, but by 1-2 volts. A LED uses this voltage drop to produce light. A LED will only light if it is connected in the right "direction".

If we parallel connect two LEDs, but in opposite directions, we'll get an interesting effect. Depending upon the direction of current, only one or the other will light. If we use a red and a green LED we can read the current's polarity at a glance. This is polarity indication in its simplest form.

LEDs are extremely sensitive for voltages over their rating of 1.5 volts. If we incorporate a resistor in the basic circuit we can drop the voltage to the LEDs and measure much higher voltages than 1.5 volts.

CONSTRUCTION

Finding a suitable casing for the probe may take a bit of searching. My casing is a large, gutted felt pen. I sawed off a piece of PC board to fit the casing and mounted the components in place. The test tip can be any solderable piece of metal of the proper form. Two holes were drilled in the case to accept the LEDs. The photo shows the test probe just prior to final assembly.

The probe has a range of 3 to 16 volts. The

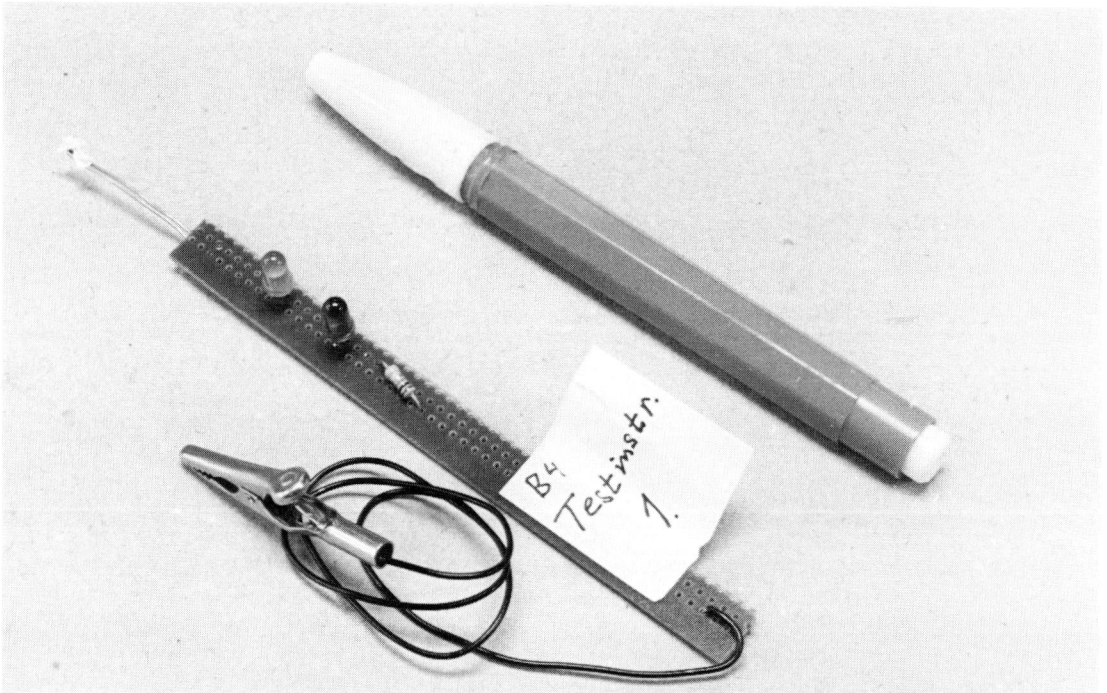

Testinstrument

D1

Green

Red

1 kohm
R1

D2

Hookupclip

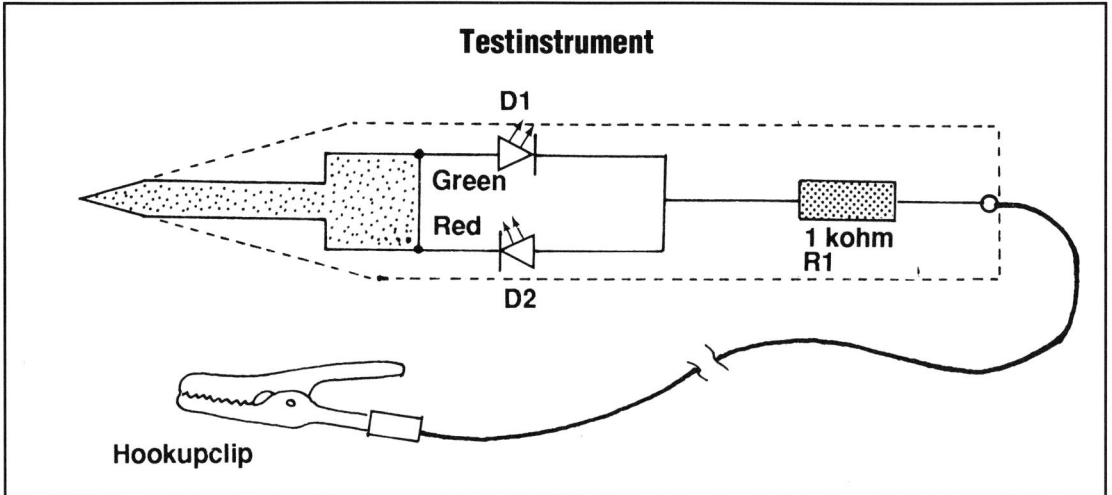

resistor is rated at 1 kΩ. Two such resistors connected in series will give you a range of 5 to 25 volts. Take your choice.

If you want both voltage ranges, add a switch to the probe so that you can choose between 1 and 2 kΩ of resistance.

USING THE PROBE
Connect the alligator clip to minus. Touch the probe to a plus. If all is well, the green LED will light.

Measuring between two pluses of the same circuit should normally give no indication in that there is normally no difference in voltage between the two. If either of the two LEDs do light, there is a diffence of at least 3 volts from one point to the other. Reverse the probe if necessary to get the green LED to light. The probe's tip now points to the higher voltage.

The probe is a great aid in tracing down layout electrical problems and you can build it for less than two dollars.

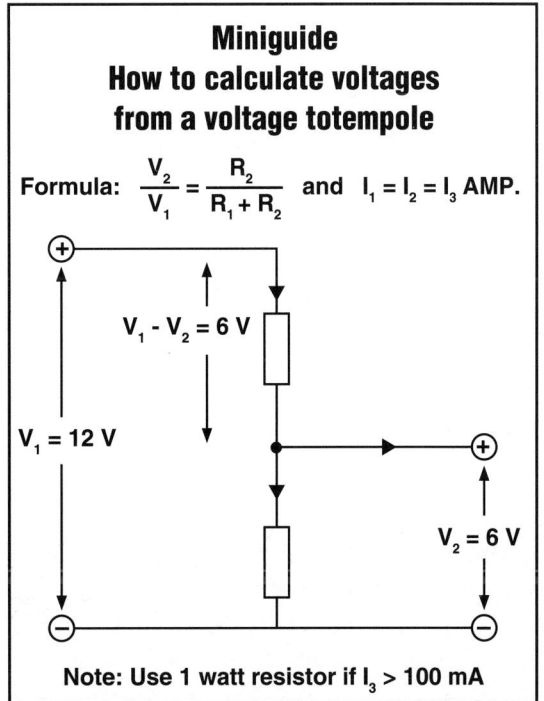

Miniguide
How to calculate voltages
from a voltage totempole

Formula: $\dfrac{V_2}{V_1} = \dfrac{R_2}{R_1 + R_2}$ and $I_1 = I_2 = I_3$ AMP.

$V_1 - V_2 = 6$ V

$V_1 = 12$ V

$V_2 = 6$ V

Note: Use 1 watt resistor if I_3 > 100 mA

Components	USA	UK
1 LED 5 mm red	276-044	1 UK58C
1 LED 5 mm green	276-022	1 UK49D
1 resistor 1 kΩ/0.5W	271-1118	1 M1K
1 experimental perfboard	276-1395	1 JP47B
1 alligator clip	270-346	1 FS56L
1 pen with soft tip*	*any supermarket	

Status indicator and reverser

To the uninitiated, this project might look like a light bulb display from General Electric. Three bulbs on one PC board may seem illogical. Especially when one is a rather large automobile bulb.

Three bulbs form this status indicator. Two of them light when an electrical fault is present in the controller circuit and the third is a locomotive speed indicator. A switch is also incorporated as a reverser.

In other chapters, we'll be building train controllers. This status indicator is intended to be connected between the controller and the track.

Operationally, the switch is the most important part of this circuit. It's used to change the polarity to the rails and thereby, a train's direction of travel.

A green light bulb is a speed indicator and translates train speed to candle power. The bulb responds to locomotive running voltages. As shown, this circuit can handle a maximum voltage of 12 to 14 volts. If you use higher voltages to run your trains, switch to higher voltage bulbs.

Hopefully, the red bulb will never light. It indicates polarity faults. This feature is especially useful if you use multiple controllers on your layout. "Power routing switches" can also cause polarity problems (those that automatically power track depending on switch position). Another potential polarity problem area is block isolation.

The third, yellow bulb is from the world of automobiles. It serves as a simple but very effective overload protector. At currents of less than one ampere (locomotives in the smaller scales seldom use more than 200 milliamps) it won't light at all. Its low

resistance will not affect train operations. If a train was to derail and cause a short circuit in the track circuit, the yellow bulb would light immediately in that it would be the only load remaining in the circuit. A lit yellow bulb is your cue to shut down the track voltage.

A practical experiment with an N scale train shows the following results. The transformer puts out 12 volts at full power. Track voltage is 11.95 volts and the current draw is 180 mA (for larger, American diesel engines). The yellow light bulb does not light. Current is restricted to 200 mA from the controller. The track is short circuited, the train stops and the light bulb glows softly. The voltage drop over the bulb is .5 volts and the current is restricted to 200 mA. When the current is permitted to rise the lamp shines successively brighter. When the short circuit is corrected the light turns off immediately and the train restarts. The

Status indicator

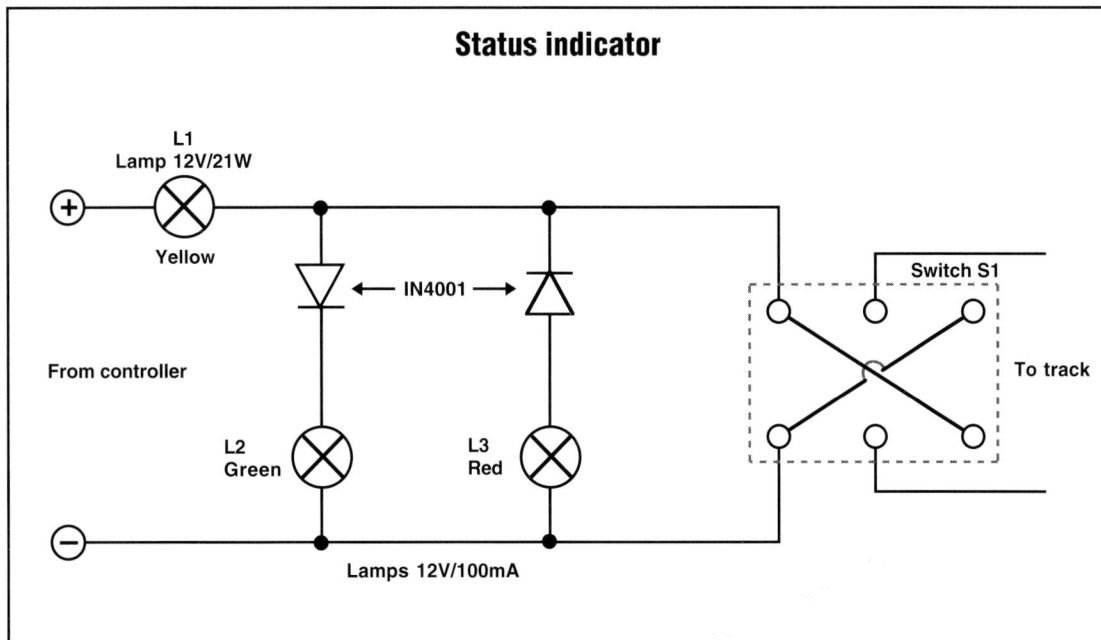

light bulb's brightness depends upon how powerful your transformer is. In this case, using a 2 A transformer, the warning light substitutes for a fuse.

CONSTRUCTION

Although this could be built on a standard circuit board a more finished look would be achieved by mounting the bulbs and switch on your control panel. The diodes could be soldered directly to the bulb sockets.

The large light bulb could be equipped with a socket. In our application the active time is rather low for each bulb. Therefore it can easily be connected to the circuit by soldering the connecting wires directly to the bulb.

Use a felt tip pen or paint to color the bulbs. For use with controllers having built in reversing switches, omit the slide switch.

CONNECTIONS

Connecting this module is simple – two wires from your controller and two to your trackwork. If your controller has a built-in reversing switch, the functions of the red and green bulbs will change depending on the direction of train travel.

Components	USA	UK
2 diodes 1N4001	276-1101	2 QL73Q
2 bulbs 12V/100 mA	272-1127	2 WL80B
1 bulb 12V/21W*	*	
2 bulb adaptors	272-357	2 RX86T
1 slide switch DPDT	275-407	1 FF77J
1 experimental perfboard	276-1395	1 JP47B
1 card-edge-connector	276-1564	1 FL86T
* Car spare bulb		

Turning loop wiring

Turning loops are nearly a must for realistic operations. Unfortunately, the electrical complications built into turning loops, often discourage beginners and veterans alike from incorporating them in their layouts. If you were to simply build a loop of track and turn on the track power, a short circuit would be 100% guaranteed.

This project will allow you to run trains through the turning loop without having to stop to change track polarity. Just throw the controller's reverser while the trains are in the loop.

The circuit will only permit trains to use the loop in one direction of travel.

The main headache with turning loops is that track polarity must change while the train is in the loop. The train is travelling back to its "old" tracks but in the opposite direction. During its trip through the loop, plus and minus have to trade places.

There are several ways to solve this problem. A feature of all of these is that both rails of the loop must be isolated from the rest of the layout's trackwork. This is usually done with plastic rail connectors.

The most common way of solving the turning loop polarity problem is by connecting a switch between the loop and the other layout trackwork. While a train is in the loop, it is brought to a complete stop, both the loop switch and controller reverser are thrown, the train is re-started and run out of the loop. More sophisticated variations use relays.

In our project, we'll be using a bridge rectifier. These are normally used to rectify

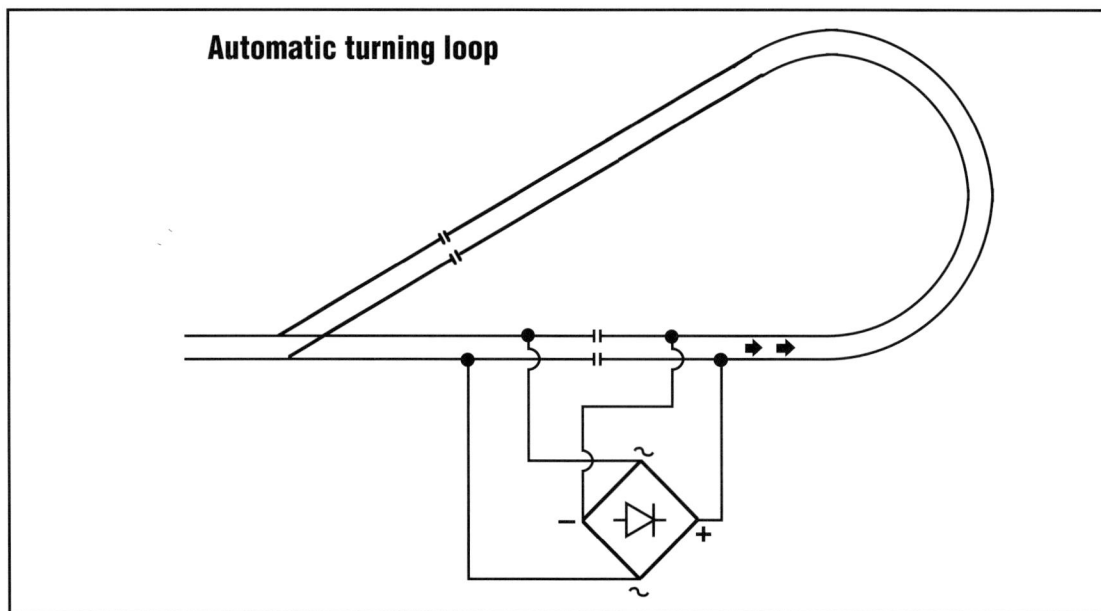

Automatic turning loop

A train never needs to stop in the turning loop as long as polarity on the rest of the layout is switched before the train leaves the loop. This can be done with a switch or automatically, with a train activated relay. If a locomotive leaves the loop block before polarity is reversed, track power will immediately short out. An additional engine length block can be added at the loop exit to eliminate this risk. Connect power leads to this extra block via diodes so that the block is only powered when polarity has been reversed. See chapter "Runaway protector" for additional details.

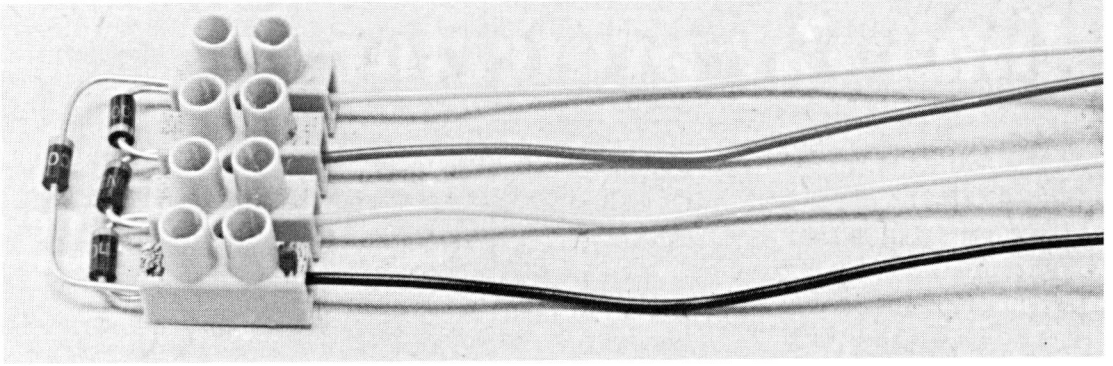

Automatic turning loop

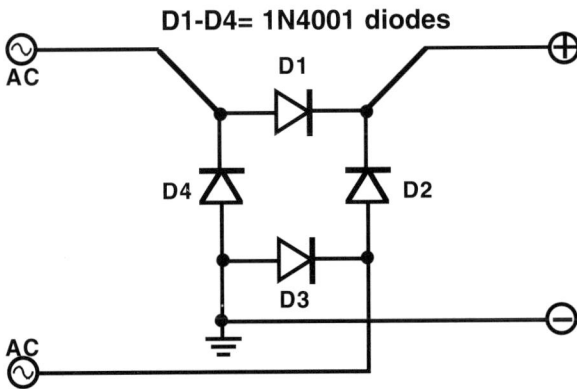

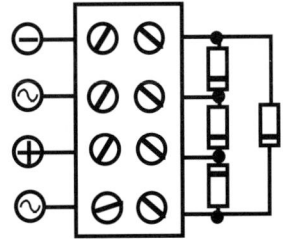

D1-D4= 1N4001 diodes

alternating current to direct current (alternating current is just a direct current that changes polarity several times per second). The rectifier will deliver a plus to the right hand rail of the loop (and allow for a forward direction of train travel) regardless of the polarity of the rest of the layout's trackwork.

CONSTRUCTION

The most simple way of constructing this project is to purchase a ready made rectifier and wire it to the loop. The connections are marked on the casing. In the interest of increasing your knowledge of electronics, you may want to build your own rectifier

using silicon diodes. The schematic shows how to connect them. Note that not all of the diodes are mounted in the same direction.

CONNECTIONS

If you haven't yet tried soldering your power leads directly to the rails, this may be the time to give it a try. Solder the leads to the outsides of the rails to prevent the solder from causing derailment problems. Practice on a piece of scrap rail. Be careful, plastic ties are easy to melt with a soldering iron. There are a few brands of rail on the market that use metal that is nearly impossible to solder to.

Components	USA	UK
4 diodes 1N4001	276-1101	4 QL73Q
1 12-way terminal block	274-679	1 FE78K

Runaway protector

This is the book's most simple project. A single diode is the only component. For those of you with lots of spurs on your layout, this modest circuit should make life a bit easier for you all.

Switching is one of the more pleasurable activities on a model railroad. For most in the hobby, running a train around and around the mainline soon loses its charm. The inclusion of freight yards and industrial spurs on a layout is very important.

This circuit will make it impossible for you to run a locomotive off the end of a spur. As soon as the engine's last right side power pickup has passed the plastic rail joiner, it also loses its running voltage. No need to pull it out by hand either. Just throw the controller in reverse and back out. This is the advantage of this diode circuit. It makes use of the fact that a diode will only let current pass in one direction.

This circuit will only work on DC layouts. If you have an AC powered Märklin layout you can easily convert to DC power. The

Miniguide
Testing transistors with an Ohm meter

PNP L / NPN H		
PNP H / NPN L		
Base (B)	Emitter (E)	
	Collector (C)	
PNP H / NPN L		
PNP L / NPN H		

	PNP H	PNP L
	NPN H	NPN L

L = Low resistance
H = High resistance

PNP-transistor — B E ex BC557 C

NPN-transistor — B C ex BC547 E

The N-scale protector

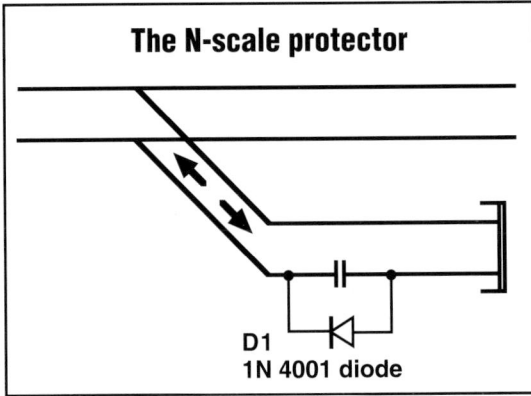

D1
1N 4001 diode

N scale locomotives are always wired so that the right hand rail is positive when the loco is run in the forward direction. H0 engines vary. If your locomotives are wired left rail positive, reverse the direction of the diode.

conversion requires only a few diodes and is described in detail in a later chapter.

If you have a hidden spur where you sometimes tuck away an extra train, this circuit is just the ticket. Traction modelers will especially find many uses for this runaway protector.

CONSTRUCTION

While the photo shows a diode soldered directly to the rail, the preferred method is to solder leads to the rail and attach the diode under the layout. Solder to the outside of the rail to avoid wheel clearance problems. Use a fine bladed saw to make the cut in the rail at the desired stopping point.

Component	USA	UK
1 diode 1N4001	276-1101	1 QL73Q

Miniguide
Calculating pulse frequence

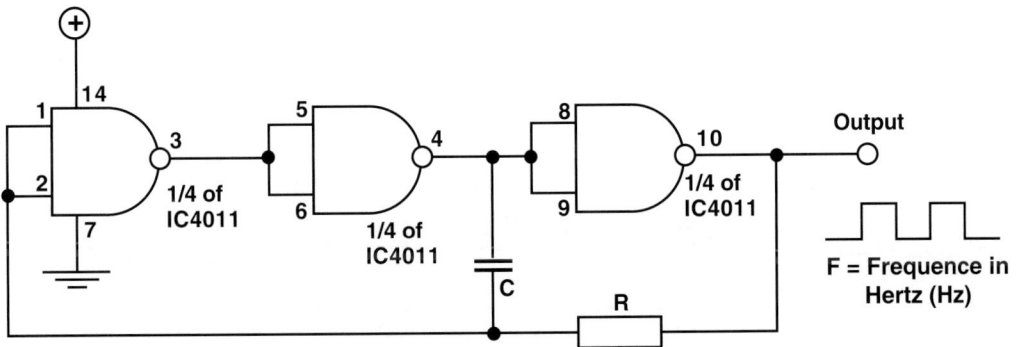

F = Frequence in Hertz (Hz)

Formula $F = \dfrac{1}{2 \times R \times C}$ Where

R is resistance in Ohms (Ω) = resistance

C is capacity in Farads (F)

Example 1:
$R = 5\ k\Omega = 5{,}000\ \Omega = 5 \times 10^3\ \Omega$
$C = 1\ \mu F = 10^{-6}\ F$

$F = \dfrac{1}{2 \times 5 \times 10^3 \times 10^{-6}} = 100\ Hz = 100$ pulses per second

Example 2:
$R = 560\ k\Omega = 560{,}000\ \Omega = 56 \times 10^4\ \Omega$
$C = 1\ \mu F$

$F = \dfrac{1}{2 \times 56 \times 10^4 \times 10^{-6}} = 0.89\ Hz$

Automatic signal

In this chapter we'll be building an automatic signal for locomotives leaving spurs. It is controlled by the locomotives forward movement and requires no form of electro-mechanical detecting switch to sense a moving train.

This signal will normally show red except for when a train is moving out of the spur. As the train starts the signal will automatically switch over to green. When the locomotive has passed the signal it will return to red.

This circuit takes advantage of the fact that an engine connects the two rails electrically even if it loses its plus voltage after passing the diode.

When the input to the signal module (the input is the lead from the track) is grounded, the signal will show red. When it's high it will show green. In all cases, except when the engine is leaving the spur, the first transistor's base is grounded via 1 kΩ

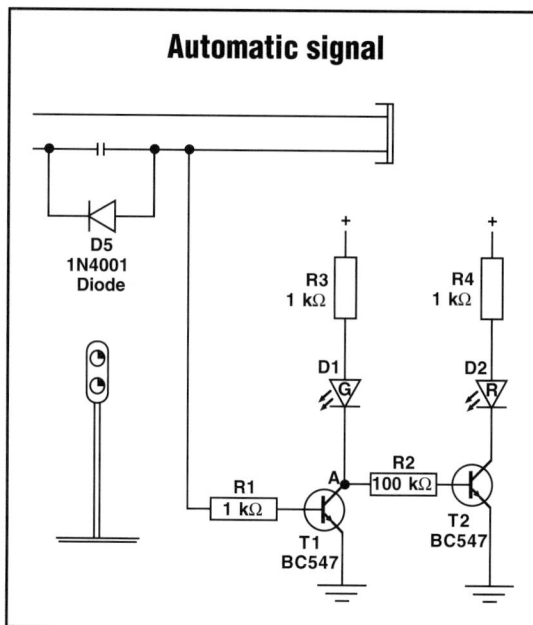

Automatic signal

resistor. Because of this, T1 is closed and the green LED can't light. At the same time, the voltage at the green LED's cathode is just above 0 volts.

**Miniguide
Regardless of how input is connected, output is correct**

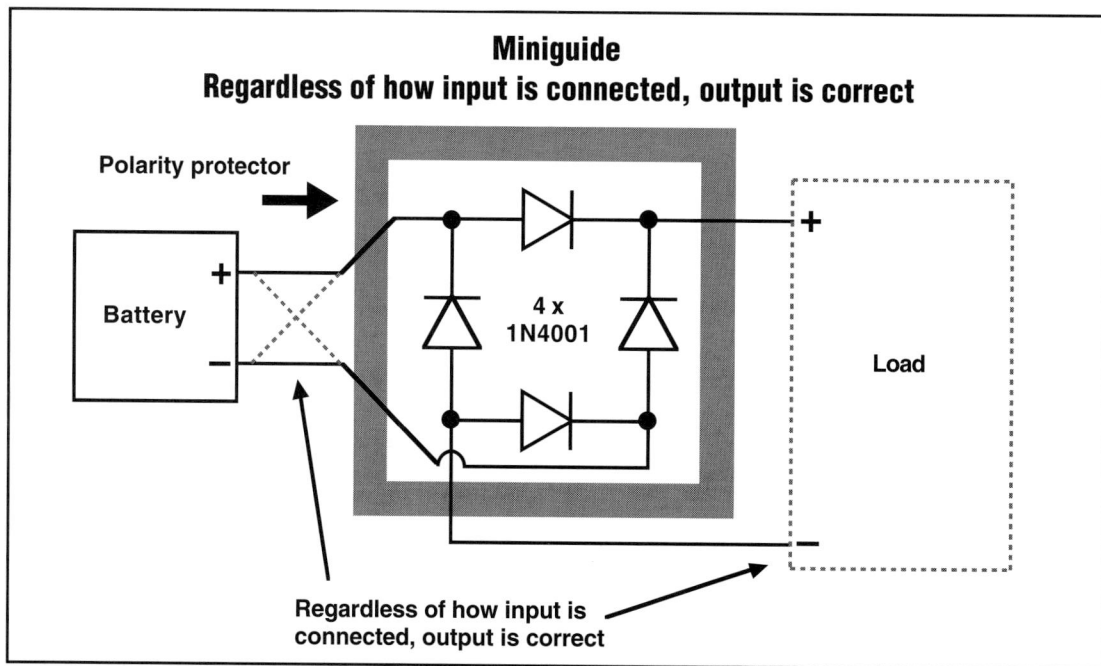

Polarity protector

Battery

4 x
1N4001

Load

Regardless of how input is
connected, output is correct

The second transistor senses this voltage at its base via a 100 kΩ resistor. This low voltage is enough to open T2. The red LED is now grounded through T2 and lights.

When a loco starts out from the siding the input receives a plus signal, opening T1 and lighting the green LED. Point A (the green LED's cathode) drops to 0 volts and T2 closes, turning off the red LED. As the engine passes the diode the module resets itself to red.

You don't have to understand the theory behind this project to build it. Despite the length of the explanation the module uses just ten components.

Point A can be used as an input for other modules. One possible application would be to connect a miniature relay to A and use it to throw the spur's switch.

CONSTRUCTION

The photo shows my prototype module. The LEDs were mounted on the circuit board for testing purposes.

CONNECTIONS

Connect the input to the rail with the diode and the two ground leads to their respective rails. Connect the module's plus to a constant 12 volt, DC power source. Use the optional point A lead as an extra control output (see output arrow on photo above).

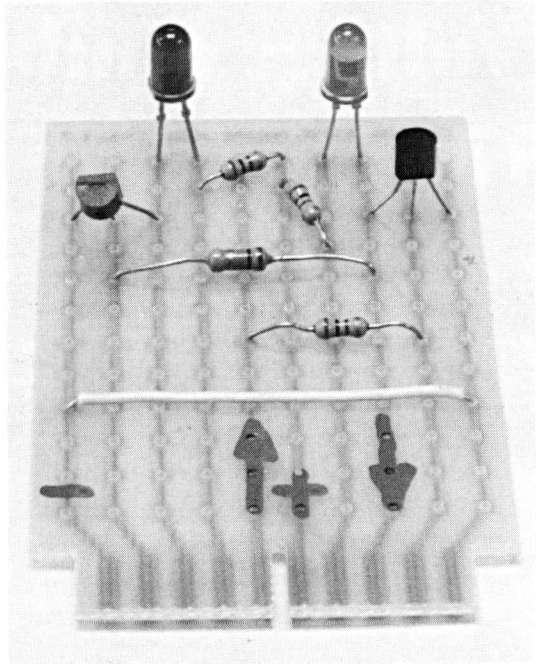

Automatic stop signal

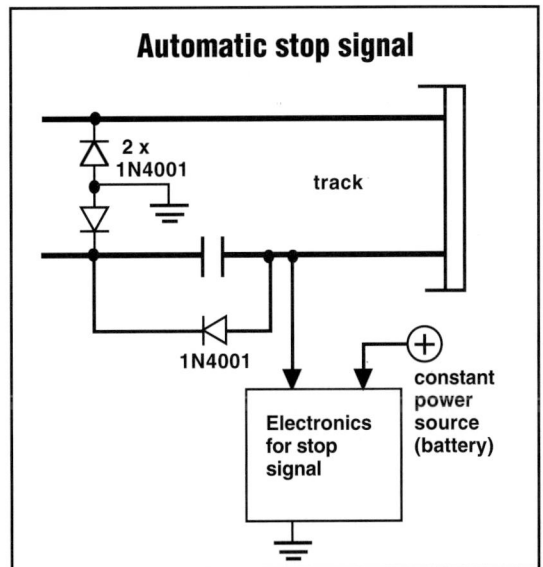

Components	USA	UK
1 LED green	276-022	1 UK49D
1 LED red	276-044	1 UK48C
2 transistors BC547	276-2009	2 QQ14Q
3 resistors 1kΩ/0.25W	271-1321	3 M1K
1 resistor 100 kΩ/0.25W	271-1347	1 M100K
1 diode 1N4001	276-1101	1 QL73Q
1 experimental perfboard	276-1395	1 JP47B
1 card-edge-connector	279-1564	1 FL86T

Voltage doubler and rectifiers

Often the power source at hand doesn't match an accessory or accessories. Some of the book's chapters deal with reducing voltage output. In this chapter we'll be looking at a way of doubling output voltages.

A light bulb can be connected to either alternating current or direct current. Most of the projects in this book are designed for DC power. Many would be destroyed if connected to an AC power source.

How is it with model locomotives? With

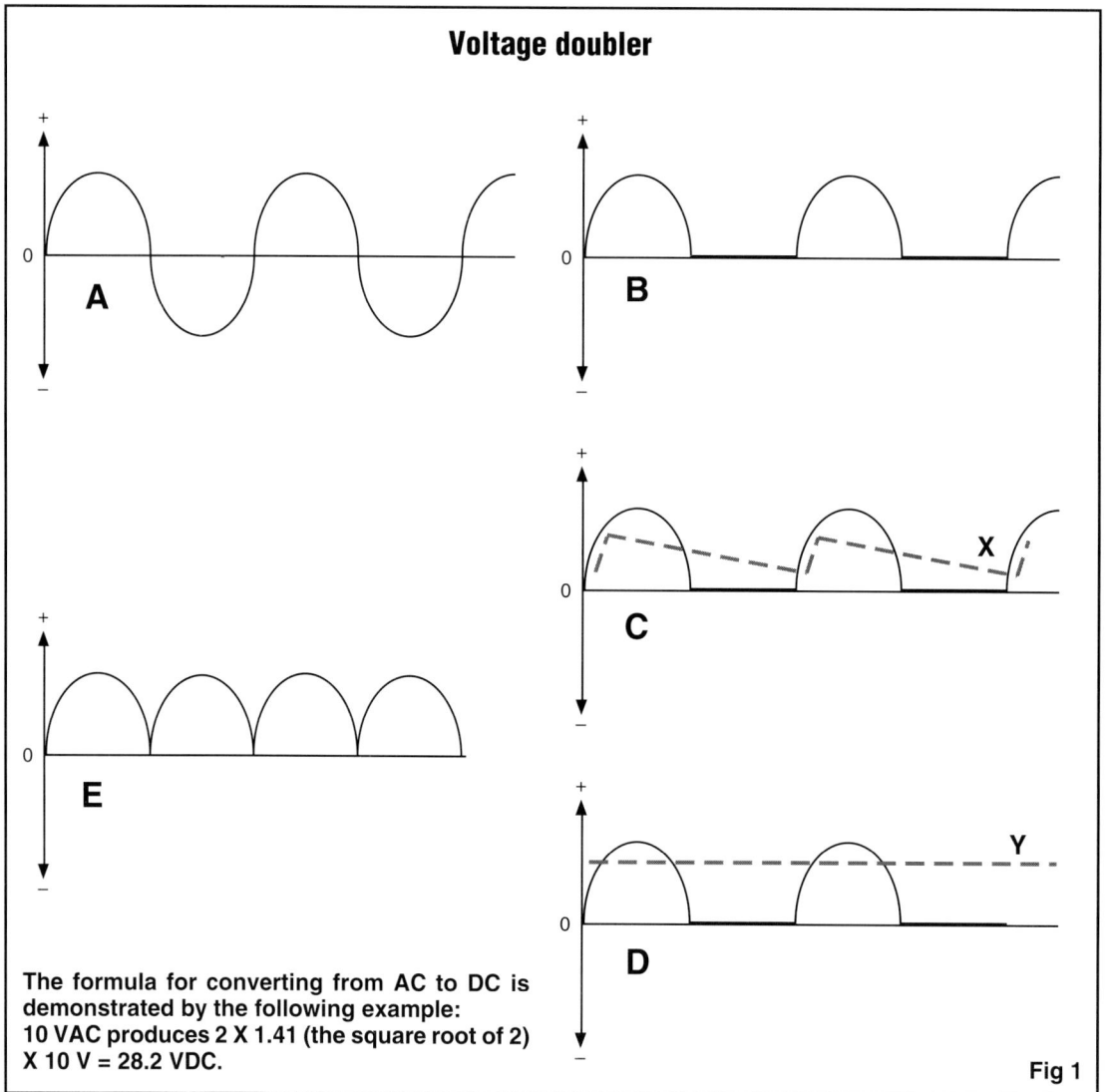

Voltage doubler

A

B

C   X

E

D   Y

The formula for converting from AC to DC is demonstrated by the following example:
10 VAC produces 2 X 1.41 (the square root of 2)
X 10 V = 28.2 VDC.

Fig 1

Voltage rectifiers

A

B

C

Fig 2

Miniguide
Switching without voltage spikes

+ 5V

10 kΩ

1 µF

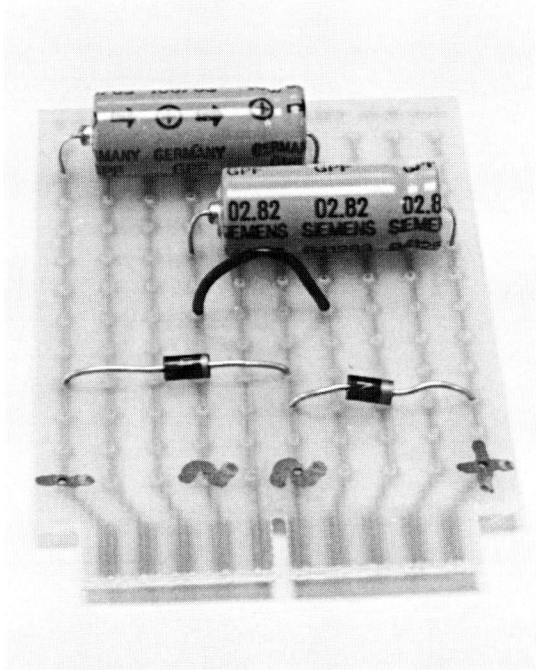

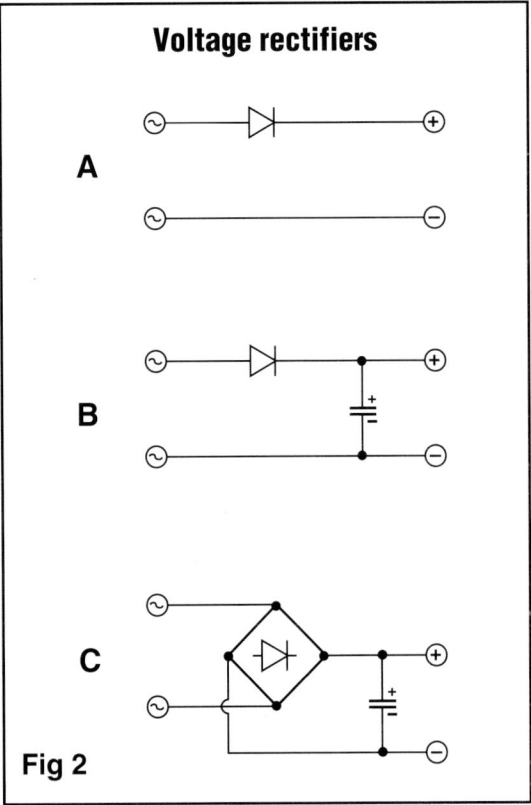

the exception of German Märklin line in Europe, Lionel O-gauge 3-rail and American Flyer S-gauge in US, all model locos run on DC (even the Märklins can be converted). Most power packs feature a variable DC outlet for train operation and an AC outlet for accessories. If the book's projects are to be powered by this outlet, you'll need to construct a rectifier. A rectifier converts AC to DC.

RECTIFIERS

Figure 1A shows an alternating current of 60 Hz.- that's 60 periods per second. A period is a positive and a negative voltage pulse. Figure 1A shows one and a half periods.

Figure 2A shows the simplest of rectifiers. It consists of one diode that only lets the positive voltage pulses pass. It delivers a pulsating direct current as shown in figure 1B.

We'll take an example. Our transformer's

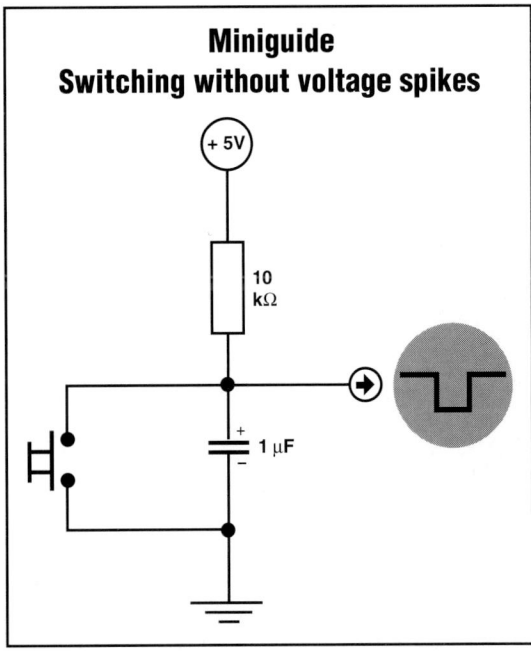

AC outlet is rated at 12 volts. This is its voltage when connectected to a load. If we were to measure directly at the outlet we

Voltage doubler

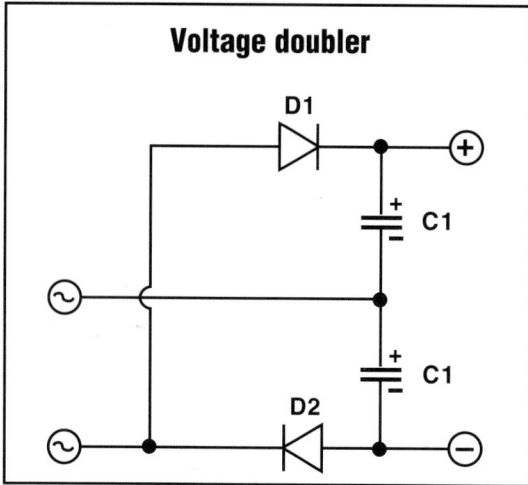

rectifying. See figure 2C. In this circuit, even the negative portion of the period is used. The output is shown in figure 1E prior to filtering (connecting the capacitor).

The same filtering as before can be accomplished with an electrolytic capacitor of half the value of that used earlier (100 µF/ 25 volts).

A suitable power source for these experiments is an AC transformer output. Do not use an unenclosed, high voltage transformer. Electrocution risk is extremely high if you do not know exactly what you are doing.

would get a reading of 13.5 volts. Connect a diode as shown in figure 2A and take a reading on the DC side (the right side). Your multimeter will show about 7 volts. Connect a 6 volt lamp to the DC output and you´ll see that the voltage has dropped to 5.8 - 6 volts. This lower voltage corresponds to figure 1C´s dashed line, marked X.

This principle is called halfwave rectifying in that the negative part of the period isn't used.

With the same basic circuit, connect a 200 µF/25 V electrolytic capacitor as shown in figure 2B. Our DC outlet voltage is now 19.2 volts. See figure D. The capacitor has evened out (or "filtered") the pulses. Connected to a load, we would have an output of 12 to 15 volts (depending on the load). The dashed line, Y, represents the filtered output voltage with a load.

If we both rectify and filter an alternating current the resulting DC voltage is the square root of 2 (about 1.41) multiplied by the AC voltage input. This is a handy bit of information and worth keeping in mind.

Finally, let's take a look at fullwave

VOLTAGE DOUBLER
The voltage doubling circuit is a halfwave rectifier with two capacitors and two diodes. Actually it's two halfwave rectifiers as described in the previous section. One rectifier takes the positive portion of the period and the other, the negative portion. Together, they will double and rectify an input voltage of 12V AC to 24V DC.

The circuit is universal in that it will work just as well on 3 volts AC as 15 volts AC. Never use AC voltages of higher than 30 volts. That's about where it starts getting dangerous.

CONSTRUCTION
We'll be using four components, as shown in the photo. Be sure to connect the capacitors in the right direction. Take a look at the section on component descriptions if you aren´t sure.

CONNECTIONS
Our voltage doubler has exactly the same connections as a fullwave bridge rectifier. After the preceeding discussion on rectifying, AC's "wave" symbol should make more sense to you now.

Components	USA	UK
2 diodes 1N4001	276-1101	2 QL73Q
2 Capacitor 100 µF/35V	272-1016	2 FB51F
1 experimental perfboard	276-1395	1 JP47B
1 card-edge-connector	276-1564	1 FL86T

A view over the Norrköping, Sweden freight yard in model form. Over 20 modern ASEA, RC locomotives are used in operations that use the same timetable as the Swedish State Railroad.

Block occupancy indicator 1

A layout indicator panel gives a picture of what's happening out on the line. It can show block occupancy, switch positions and more.

For train position indication, the layout must be divided into blocks and each block equipped with a detector. In this chapter we'll be looking at a basic detector. For a more elaborate detector, see the following chapter.

This chapter's single directional detector will not be harmed by bi-directional train movements – it just won't detect.

HOW IT WORKS

The schematic shows one rail isolated from the surrounding trackwork. The block power switch is included in the schematic.

A 1 kΩ resistor was selected for use with a 12-14 volt controller. If you are working in Z scale, where 7 volt controllers are the norm, use a 680 Ω resistor instead.

As long as the block is unoccupied, the detector is ungrounded and the LED will

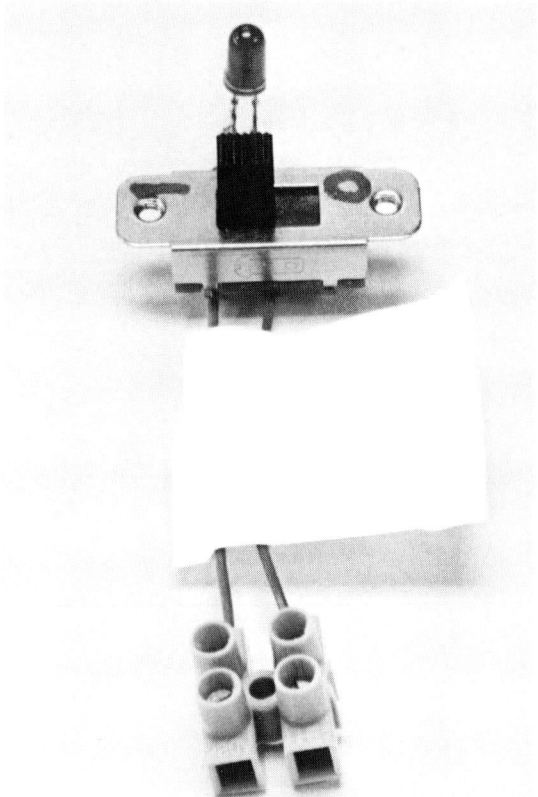

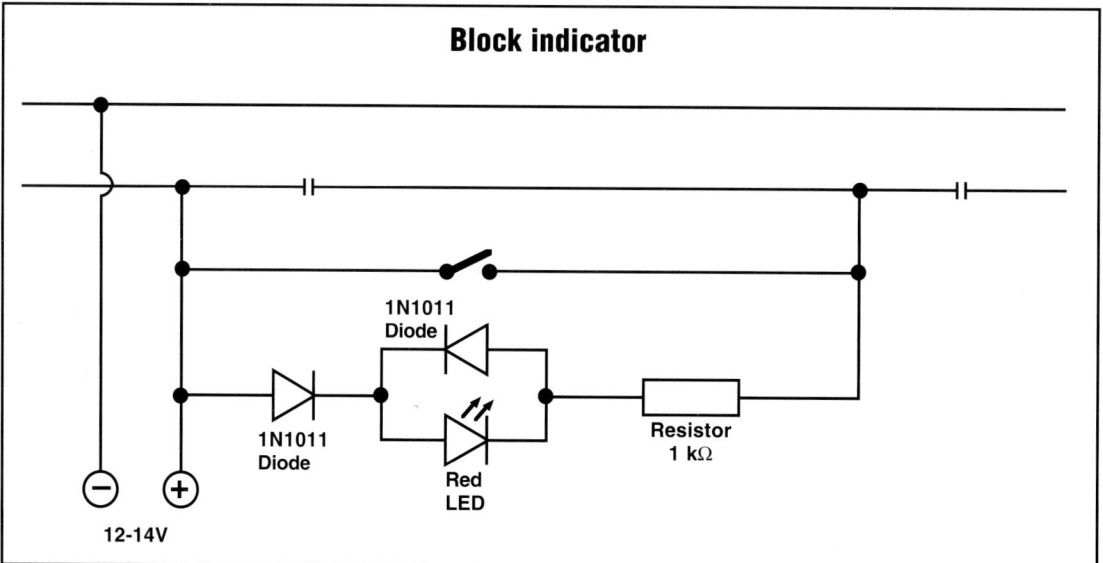

Block indicator

1N1011
Diode

1N1011
Diode

Red
LED

Resistor
1 kΩ

12-14V

not light. If the block power switch is on, the detector will have a plus at both ends and won't light in this case either – even if a train passes through the block.

This very basic circuit detects a train when it has stopped in the block, the block power switch is in the off position, the controller reverser is properly set and the controller is powering the preceeding block. In this case and this case only, the circuit is grounded via the engines wheels and motor and the LED will light.

For those of you that wish to develop this circuit further you can replace the switch with a relay. The relay can be controlled by the preceeding block. The result is automatic train control.

CONSTRUCTION

In the interest of space conservation, the components can be soldered directly to the switch terminals. A circuit board is unnecessary.

The switch terminals serve as soldering points for the three, serial connected components. As you can see in the photo, the LED`s legs have been bent at 90 degree angles. Bend carefully using a pair of small, long nose pliers to avoid cracking the plastic case.

To ease installation the module is supplied with connecting wires and a 12-way terminal block. Terminal blocks can be shortened as required.

CONNECTIONS

If you plan to incorporate a series of detectors on your layout use terminal strips. It will simplify connections and make for neater wiring.

Miniguide Voltage switch

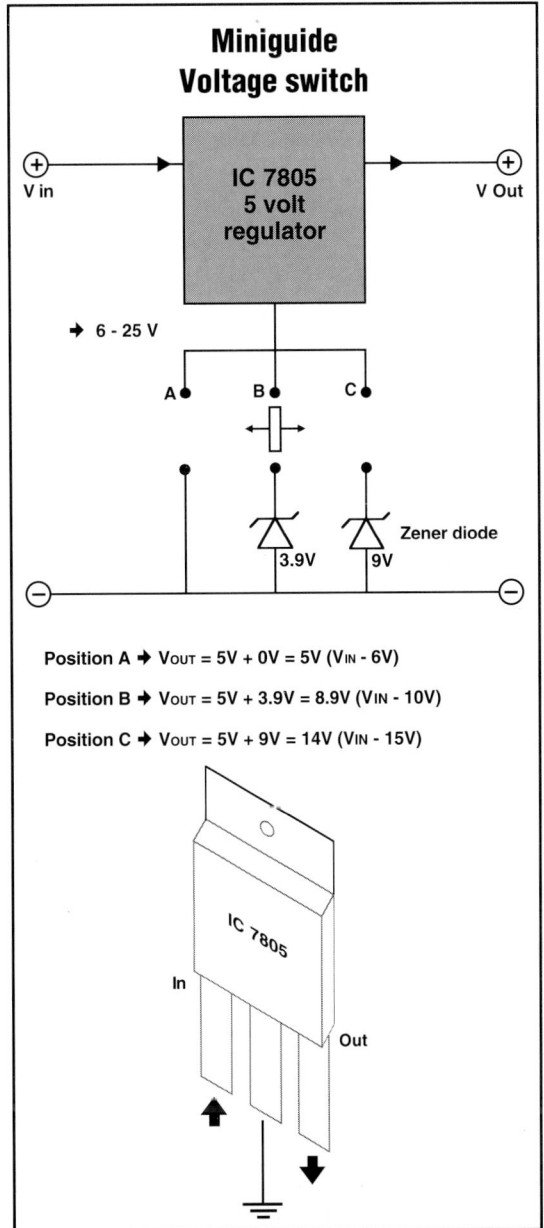

Position A → V_{OUT} = 5V + 0V = 5V (V_{IN} - 6V)

Position B → V_{OUT} = 5V + 3.9V = 8.9V (V_{IN} - 10V)

Position C → V_{OUT} = 5V + 9V = 14V (V_{IN} - 15V)

Components	USA	UK
1 diode 1N4001	276-1101	1 QL73Q
1 LED red 5 mm	276-044	1 UK48C
1 resistor 1 kΩ/0.25W	271-1321	1 M1K
1 slide switch SPST	275-406	1 FF77J
1 12-way terminal block	274-679	1 FE78K

Block occupancy indicator 2

If your trackage is divided into separate control blocks, a block indication system is very useful. It will allow you to follow the train movements from your control panel. This chapter covers a more advanced version of the single directional indicator from the preceeding chapter. This indicator is bi-directional.

As in the basic version, it only indicates when the block power switch is in the off position and the preceeding block is powered.

Let's begin by looking at the difference between these two similar circuits.

This circuit is bi-directional thanks to the incorporation of a bridge rectifier. It allows the circuit to work regardless of which rail is plus or minus. The rectifiers secondary side (marked with a plus and a minus sym-

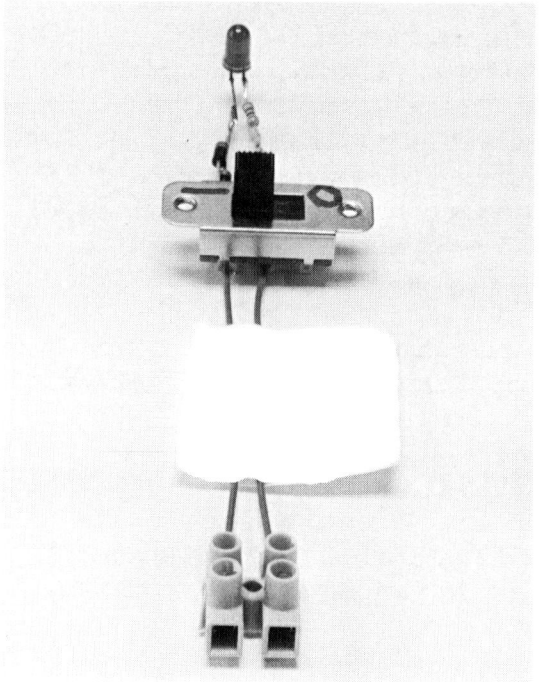

Block indicator

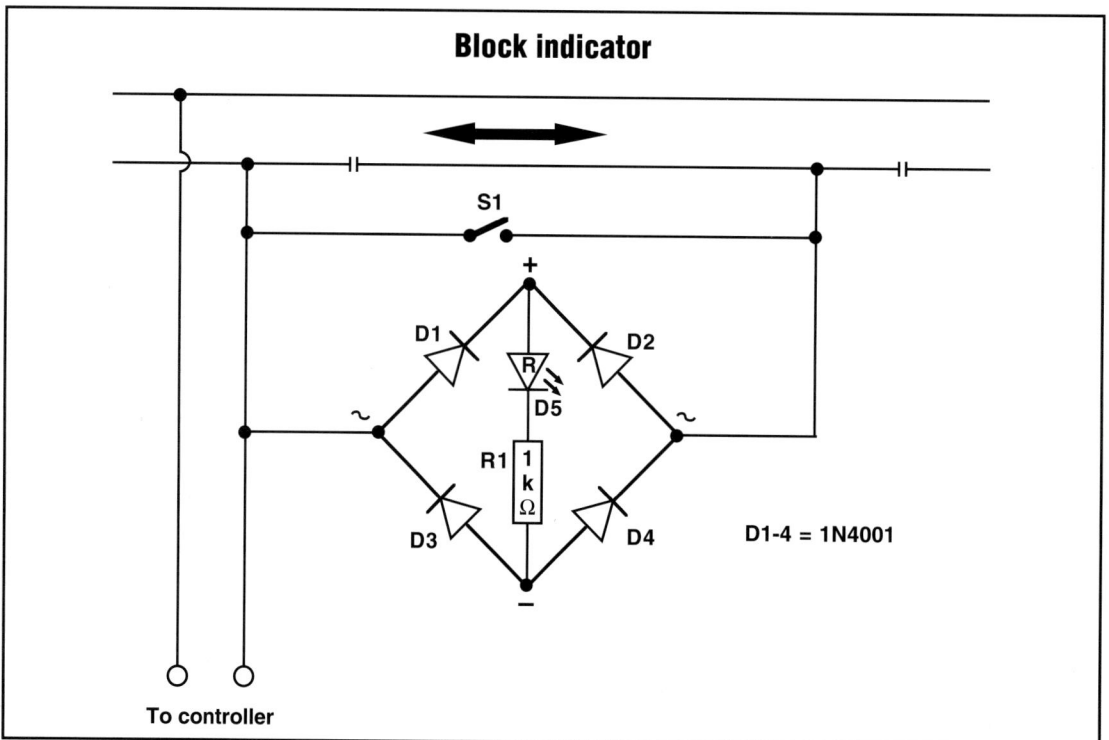

S1

D1   D2
R
D5
R1 1 k Ω
D3   D4   D1-4 = 1N4001

To controller

**Miniguide
Using ICs as relay drivers**

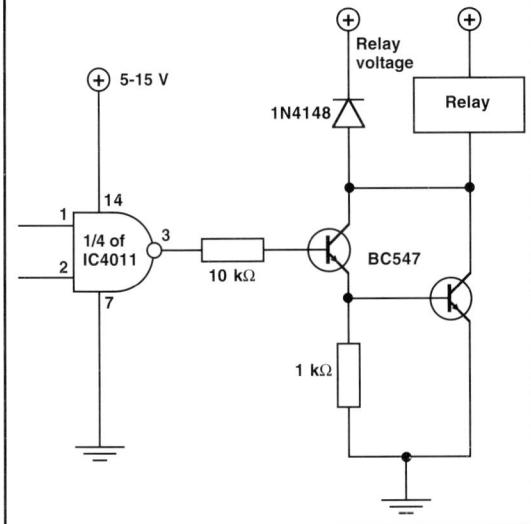

**Miniguide
Using ICs as lamp and led drivers**

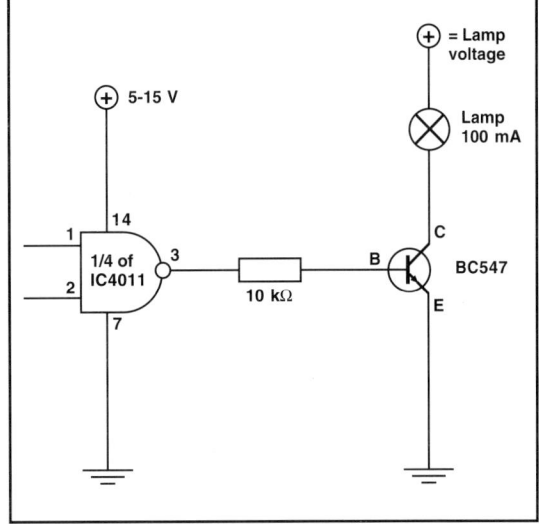

bol on its casing) always delivers a voltage of the correct polarity – even when the polarity changes on the primary side (marked with AC's wave symbol).

Despite the slight voltage drop of .6 volts over the rectifier's diodes, full track power would soon burn out the LED if it wasn't for the 1 KΩ resistor in this circuit (as in the preceeding chapter, 680 Ω is a suitable resistor for Z scale applications). The LED will light at full strength at 12 volts. Even at a controller voltage of just 3 - 3.5 volts (2 to 2.5 volts in Z scale), the LED will still glow strong enough to see.

CONSTRUCTION

As in the single directional unit, the components can be mounted directly to the block power switch.

While an integrated rectifier (all of the diodes are integrated in a single housing) can be used, I chose to use separate diodes. The diodes can be mounted on a circuit board.

CONNECTIONS

Connecting the module leads to the layout is simple - look at the schematic.

This is a good time to take up LED mounting. The crude way is to just drill a hole in your panel, push it in and squish in a little glue to keep it from falling out. The right way is to use plastic LED holders. Drill a 1/4" (6.5 mm) hole. The holder is a two-piece affair. Push the ring with the smallest diameter (it has a collar) in the hole from the front. Push the remaining ring over the LED and press them back into the first ring, from the rear. You'll probably have to use a small screwdriver to get them in the last little bit. With holders, you'll get a professional look, won't have to mess with glue and if you ever need to change the LED, you won't need a hammer and punch to get it out.

Components	USA	UK
4 diodes 1N4001	276-1101	4 QL73Q
1 LED red 5 mm	276-044	1 UK48C
1 resistor 1 kΩ/0.25W	271-1321	1 M1K
1 slide switch SPST	275-406	1 FF77J
1 12-way block terminal	274-679	1 FE78K

Pulse generator

In this chapter we'll be building a little unit that will help us start and stop our locos at realistic speeds.

The module is designed for use between the transformer and a controller that we will be constructing in a later chapter.

Does the following sound familiar? You carefully increase track power but nothing happens. Your train is standing still. Suddenly it starts but at a too high rate of speed. It´s not that the locomotive is incapable of slow speed operations – reducing power will prove that. The problem is that the locomotive has a friction threshold that must be overcome before it can start. The motor´s start resistance is greater than its rotation resistance.

The better and usually more expensive model locomotives come equipped with five and sometimes seven pole motors. At the other end of the scale are the three pole motors. The more poles a motor has, the smoother it will start. If it's prototypical starts you're after, begin by stocking your railroad with good quality motive power.

The next step is to keep your rails clean. If you have dirty rails, you'll know by those sudden, unscheduled stops your trains are making. Periodic cleaning will do wonders for your train movements.

Now to controllers...the better ones are expensive but are excellent products. They are usually equipped with special, slow speed circuits. The advertisements often make mention of pulse power. This chapter's project, when used with a later chapter's controller, will give you pulse power at a fraction of the cost of the ready made controllers.

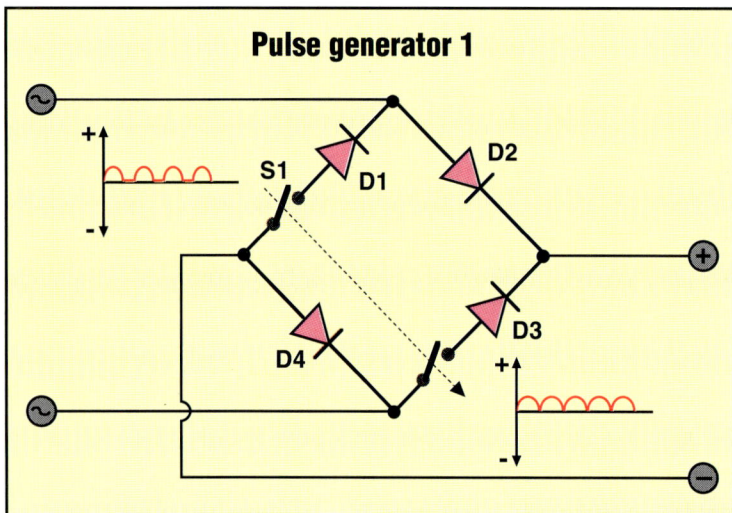

Pulse generator 1

Components	USA	UK
4 diodes 1N4001	276-1101	4 QL73Q
1 slide switch SPST	275-406	1 FF77J
1 experimental perfboard	276-1395	1 JP47B
1 card-edge-connector	276-1564	1 FL86T

HOW IT WORKS

For normal operations our pulse power will come from a full wave rectifier. See the schematic. When slow speed operation is required, a throw of a two pole, single throw switch will convert the fullwave rectifier to a halfwave rectifier.

With the switch in the halfwave position, the motor only gets a pulse half as often as in the fullwave position. In that each pulse moves the motor's rotor a bit, sending out pulses only half as often makes for much slower and smoother starts than otherwise possible. For normal, mainline running the switch is returned to the fullwave position. Motors run a little cooler on fullwave voltages.

CONSTRUCTION

You can build this circuit on a PC board, mount it in a handheld controller or even put it on a control panel with the diodes soldered directly to the switch - whatever works best for you.

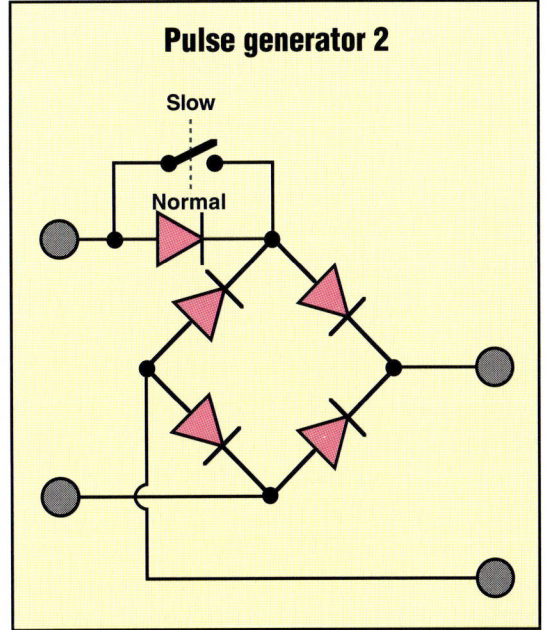

Pulse generator 2

Slow

Normal

CONNECTIONS

The module has two AC inputs and two DC outputs and is connected the same as a common rectifier. The DC outputs must be connected so that plus doesn't go to ground (minus) on the accompanying module.

Automatic dimmer

In an earlier chapter we built a simple, manual dimmer switch. This time we'll be building a more advanced version - one that automatically regulates the voltage to our LEDs and lamps. The level of light in the train room determines how bright they'll shine.

A lamp or LED equipped control panel can be distracting in low light level conditions. On the other hand, the same control panel may be hard to read when the lights are turned up. Light points that vary intensity in proportion to room lighting is preferable.

This circuit can handle an output of 200 mA – that's four 50 mA bulbs or about 20 LEDs. The individual lights share a common ground through the integrated circuit (IC or chip).

Miniguide

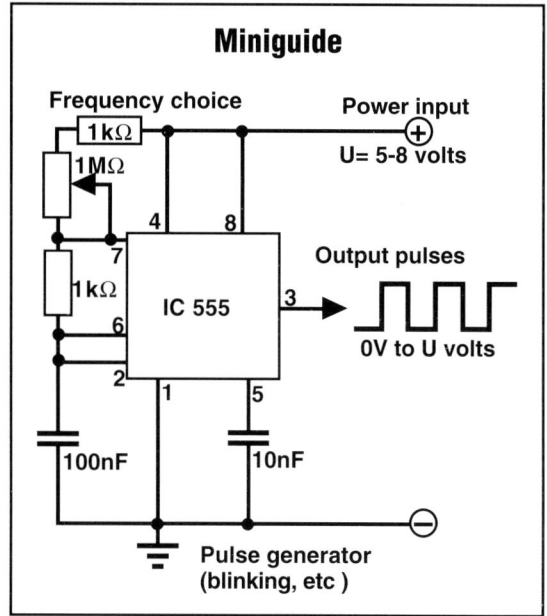

Frequency choice

1kΩ

1MΩ

1kΩ

IC 555

100nF

10nF

Power input
U= 5-8 volts

Output pulses

0V to U volts

Pulse generator
(blinking, etc)

HOW IT WORKS
Our chip is the much used IC 555. It's an oscillator whose frequency can be varied by resistors and capacitors. The resistors at pin 7 determine the charging time for the

Automatic dimmer

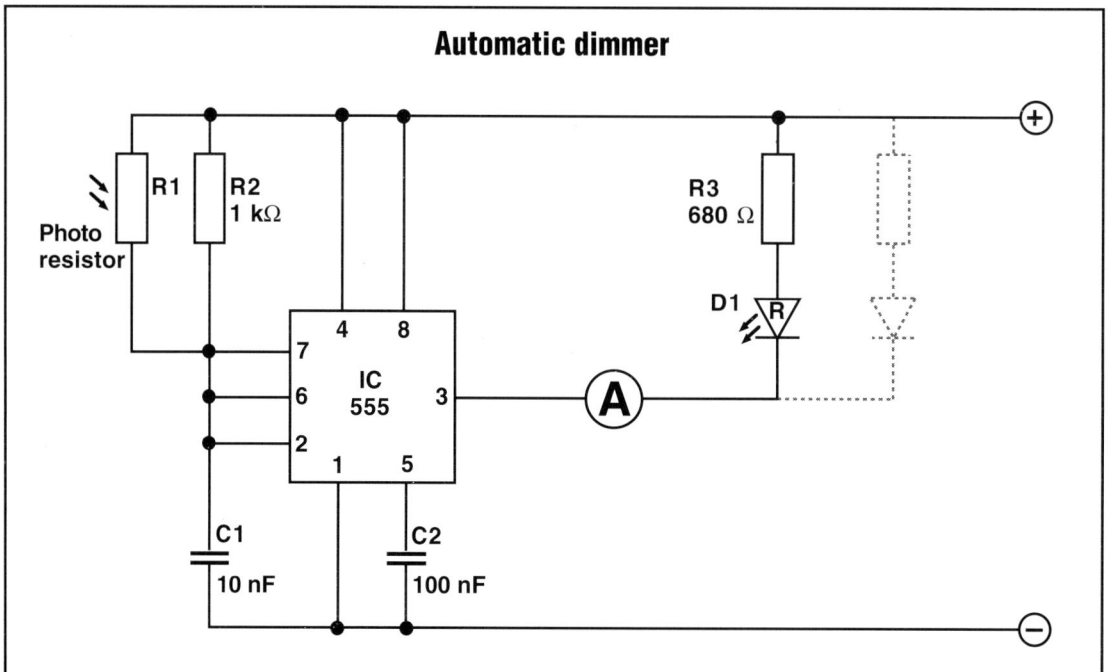

Photo resistor

R1

R2
1 kΩ

R3
680 Ω

IC
555

D1

C1
10 nF

C2
100 nF

A

CO-22-1421

capacitor at pin 2 which in turn determines the frequence at pin 3. This variable frequence of pulses at pin 3 range from full voltage to grounded, with nothing in between ("1" or "0" are the terms used in electronics for this all or nothing situation).

By using a photoresistor at pin 7 we can allow the level of light in our train room decide the frequence at pin 3. The more light the photo resistor is exposed to, the longer pin 3 is "low" and the brighter our lamps and LEDs will shine. Substitute the photoresistor for a 10 kΩ potentiometer and you'll get a manual dimmer.

CONSTRUCTION
See the section on component descriptions for IC 555's pin numbering (it's not the same as shown on the schematic).

Lay out the components as shown in the photo to minimize altering the PC board more than necessary. You can mount the photoresistor in a tube to make it more directional. Direct it towards the ceiling lights or a special spotlight.

CONNECTIONS
On my module I've mounted a LED and its accompanying resistor. This is for demonstration purposes only. Your own LEDs and lamps will be connected to the module via leads from your control panel or from the layout proper.

Power to the automatic dimmer can vary from 5 volts to 12 volts.

Components	USA	UK
1 Timer-IC 555	276-1723	1 QH66W
1 resistor 1 kΩ/0.25W	271-1321	1 M1K
1 resistor 680 Ω/0.25W	271-1117	1 M680Ω
1 capacitor 0.1 µF	272-135	1 YR75S
1 capacitor 0.01 µF	272-131	1 BX00A
1 photoresistor 50 MΩ	276-1657	1 HB10L
1 LED red 5 mm	276-044	1 QL73Q
1 experimental perfboard	276-1395	1 JP47B
1 card-edge-connector	276-1564	1 FL86T

Steam whistle

Most of the projects in this book deal with either controlling train movements or by contributing to the layout's feeling of life and activity by regulating light. With electricity we can also create sound.

This whistle won't create a concert but adds a nice touch for those of you that run steam engines on your layout. With modern electronics we can imitate just about any sound imaginable. The better synthesizers, for example, can simulate any musical instrument.

We'll be building this steam whistle simulator with two transistors, one resistor, a potentiometer, a capacitor, a loudspeaker and a battery (for on-board mounts). The semiconductors will produce an alternating current that the speaker will transform into sound. The sound is adjusted by varying the resistance to T1 by turning the potentiometer. The whistle's on/off switch can be a push-button for layout mounted modules or a magnetically controlled relay for on-board mounts.

See the chapter on diesel horns for some additional thoughts on on-board applications.

CONSTRUCTION

Before beginning construction you are going to have to make a decision. Are you going to mount the module on the train or on the layout? You can build the module to fit on most H0 locos, but in N and Z scales things can get pretty tight. If you can't find space in the locomotive or tender you may consider mounting it in one of your cars.

The largest components in this circuit are the speaker and the battery. They may well make the decision for you in whether you should build an on-board module or not. The photo shows a small speaker from a headphone set. While they may not give the best sound, they are small and a reasonable alternative to a full size speaker.

If you can't fit this circuit into your engines, all is not lost. Mount the circuit board under the layout and tuck the speaker away in the scenery. You'll be able to

Miniguide – Sound generator

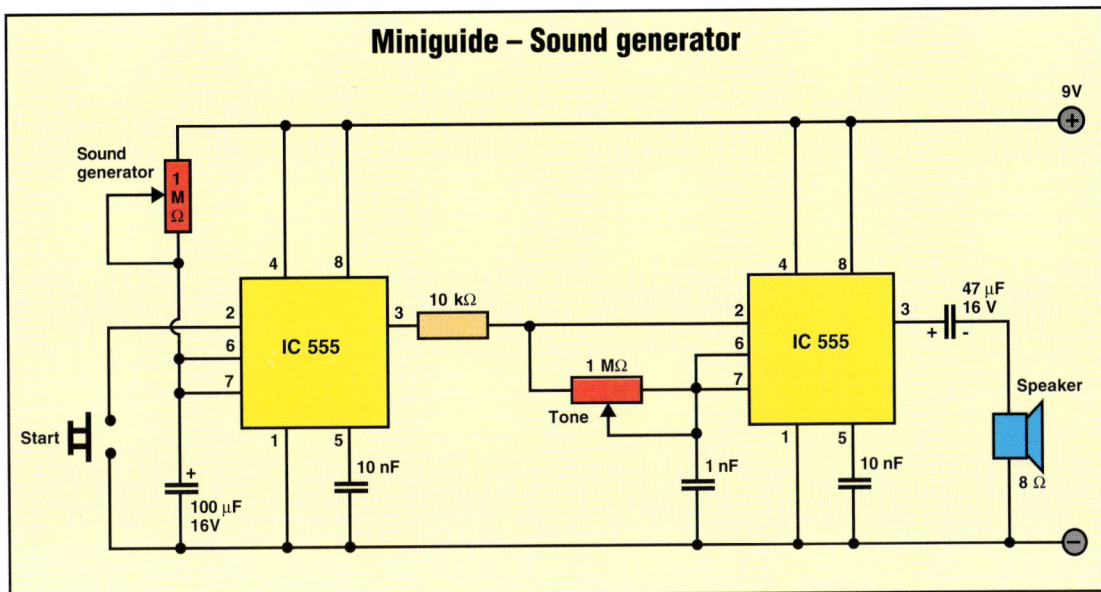

use a full size speaker and that means better sound quality.

Connect the trimpotentiometers middle leg to T1 and one of the outer two to plus. The third can be soldered in place for stability purposes but don't connect it electrically. The speaker leads will stay put better with a few drops of ACC glue in addition to the solder.

CONNECTIONS

Your power source can either be a battery (or batteries) or a DC outlet in the 9 volt to 12 volt range.

For the layout mount version the whistle's on/off switch can be a push-button. For automatic operation, home-made, wheel activated, miniature switches or reed switches can be used. In the latter case, mount small magnets on your engines' underframes to draw the switches. For a series of whistles just use more switches.

For on-board mounts we'll have to turn things around

Steam whistle

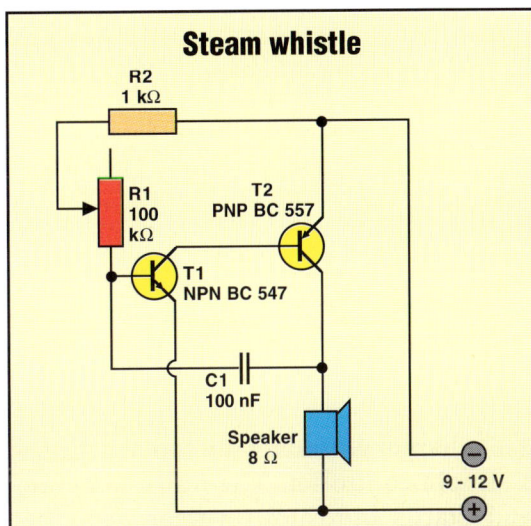

a bit. Mount the reed switches under the locos (don't worry, they're small) and the magnets in the trackwork. Kadee uncoupler magnets would be ideal.

Components	USA	UK
1 transistor BC557	276-2023	1 QQ16S
1 transistor BC547	276-2009	1 QQ14Q
1 capacitor 0.1 µF	272-135	1 YR75S
1 miniature variable resistor 100K	271-284	1 UHØ6G
1 experimental perfboard	276-1395	1 JP47B
1 card-edge-connector	276-1564	1 FL86T
1 loudspeaker 8 Ω	40-245	1 YT25C

Controller

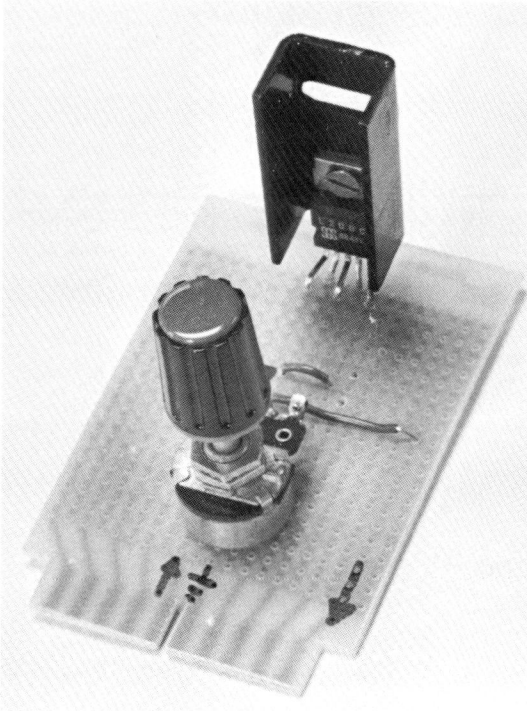

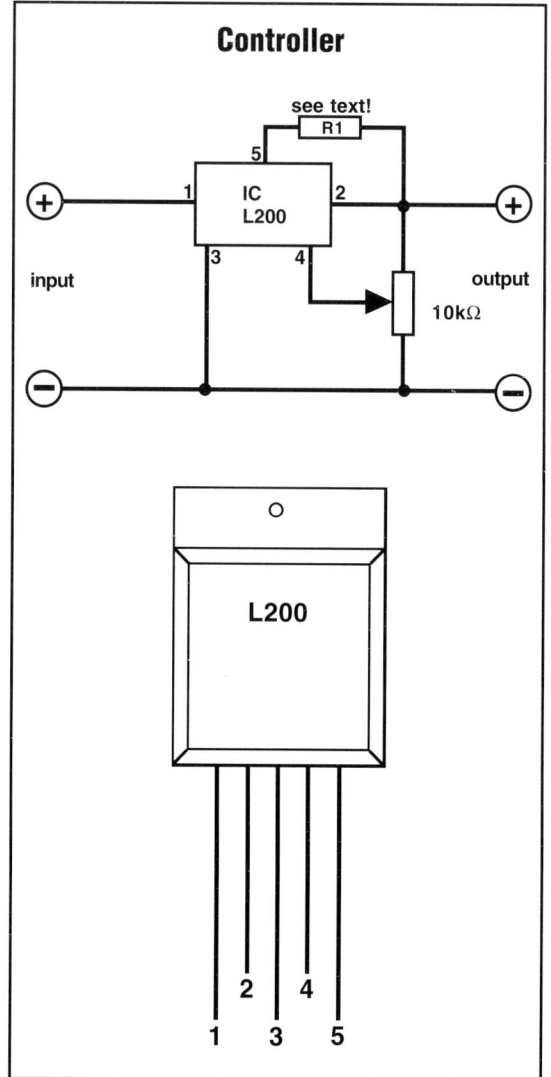

This chapter will cover the construction of a simple controller. The pulse generator and status indicator/reverser described earlier are to be connected to this controller module.

HOW IT WORKS

To make this project as simple as possible, I have selected a "smart" IC that does most of the voltage regulating internally. It's an L200 and it is a voltage regulator with built-in overload and overheating protection. It'll disconnect current in overload situations (short circuits) and stay that way until the fault is corrected. This is a component that normally runs a bit warm. That's why it has

the overheating protection feature and why we'll be using a heat sink. We can either dissipate the heat with a bolt-on heat sink or by attatching it to a metal enclosure case.

The IC will regulate voltages from 2.85 volts up to 36 volts. In HO and N scales I haven't had any problems getting a loco-motive to come to a complete stop at 2.85 volts. Z scale is another story. To further drop the voltage, connect a diode or diodes at the plus output. Each diode will drop the voltage by .6 volts.

As long as the L200 is connected, properly it is foolproof. Within its casing it contains 33 transistors and six diodes. Now you know why they call them "integrated circuits".

The only external components on this module is the potentiometer and a resistor. If you prefer, a slide-type potentiometer can be used. The resistor value (R1) should be 0.5 Ω (1 watt) if max output is 1 amp. Change it to 0.22 Ω (2 watts) if max output is 2 amps.

CONSTRUCTION

You may find that the IC's legs don't quite match up with the holes on your circuit board. It's OK to bend them to fit, just be careful.

Save yourself a little work and combine the minuses of the output and input. Any reduction in total connections reduces the chances of problems later and helps keep the "snakes" at bay.

CONNECTIONS

Between the output and the tracks connect the status indicator/reverser module from the earlier chapter. Tap the pulse generator in just before the reverser switch.

Connect the input to the AC output of your power pack via a rectifier. The controller itself will work just fine connected to a DC outlet but you'll be needing that AC for the pulse generator module.

TROUBLESHOOTING

Problems? Check your soldering. Any bad connections? A cold soldering perhaps? Maybe a bit of solder has inadvertantly run over and caused a short. Is everything connected correctly? Although it is extremely rare, you'll sometimes come across a component with a manufacturing fault. Not to be rude, but if it doesn't work, you've probably made a construction error. It happens to the best of us. Just keep a cool head and trace it down logically.

If you have had problems, run the repaired controller on "idle" before connecting it to your trackage. By this, I mean that the inputs are connected as usual but the outputs are connected to a voltmeter. The voltmeter should show a voltage (use the meter`s DC scale) that varies as the potentiometer is turned.

Components	USA	UK
1 IC-chip L200 *		1 YY74R
1 potentiometer 10 kΩ	271-1721	1 JM71N
1 heat sink for L200 **	6030B	1 FG52G
1 experimental perfboard	276-1395	1 JP47B
1 card-edge-connector	276-1564	1 FL86T
* order LM317 (276-1778) if L200 is n.a.		
** Jameco order No.		

Chase lights

There's nothing quite like chase lights for getting folks' attention. And this is true whether it's the "real world" we're talking about or our model railroads.

In another chapter we constructed a circuit that would blink a chain of lights in unison. This chase light circuit is much more difficult to build. I wouldn't suggest it as a first project for a beginner.

Two applications for this project come to mind. As part of a sign (either as a pillar of light or as a frame to the sign) or as a part of a highway construction warning system.

Although the schematic shows the basic circuit with just eight LEDs you can run up to 24 LEDs with additional components.

HOW IT WORKS

The "brains" in this circuit are two IC chips of the CMOS type (Complementary Metal Oxid Semiconductor). Take a look at the schematic. IC1 is an oscillator – a timer in other words. It determines how fast the LEDs will "chase". As designed, this circuit's blink frequency can be set from .75 Hz. to so fast that you can't see that the LEDs are blinking anymore. The speed is set by the trim potentiometer (trimmer).

The timer, IC1 steers IC2, a counter chip. IC2 is constructed so that it will only light one LED at a time. Think of it as counting in a ring, sending out signals to the LEDs, one at a time. The first in the rotation won't light again until the last one has turned off.

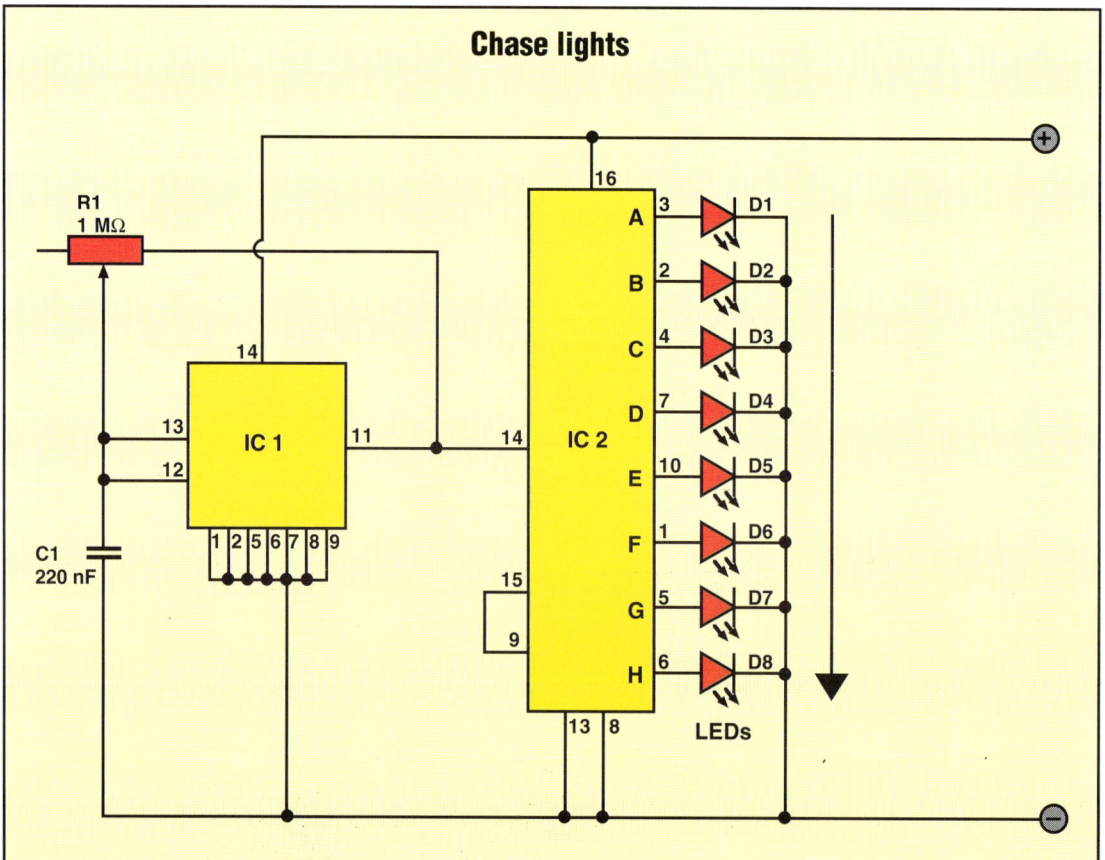

Chase lights

R1 1 MΩ

C1 220 nF

IC 1

IC 2

D1 D2 D3 D4 D5 D6 D7 D8

LEDs

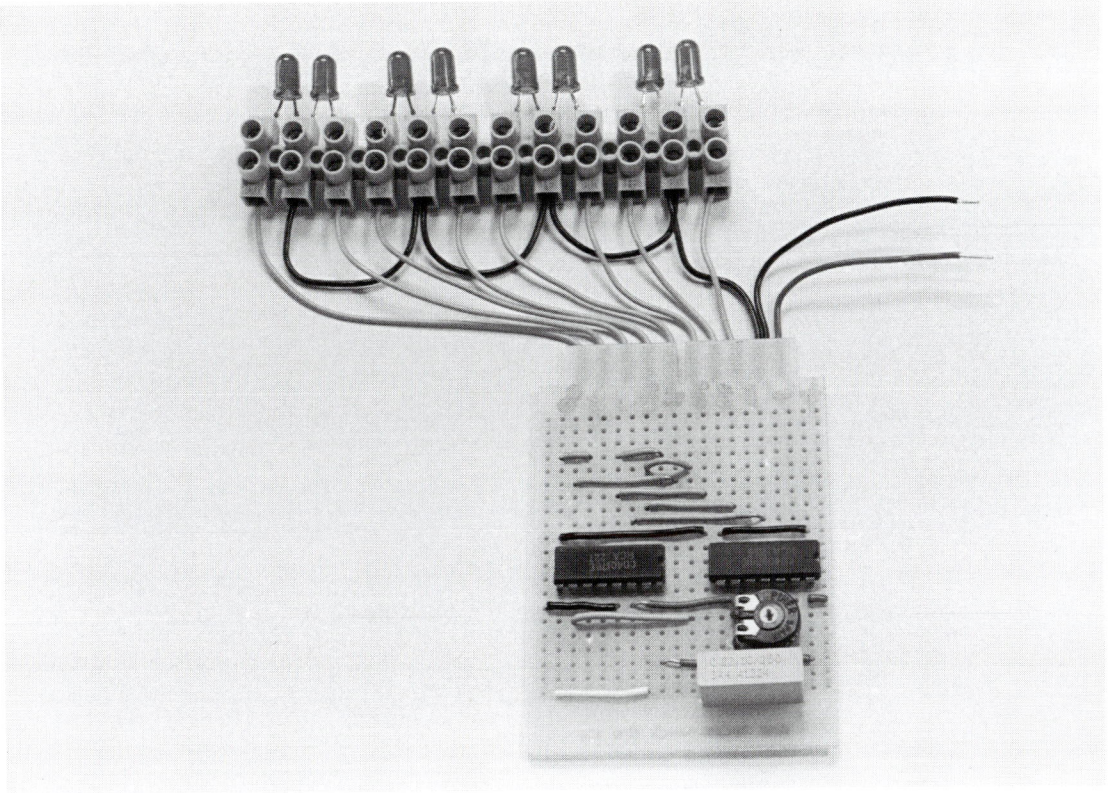

You may have noticed all of the grounded pins on IC1. When working with CMOS chips, unconnected pins are to be avoided. If they aren't to be used, connect all unused pins to minus.

IC1 could be replaced with a 555 timer. It also works as an oscillator but please observe that it uses a different pin arrangement than the CMOS IC.

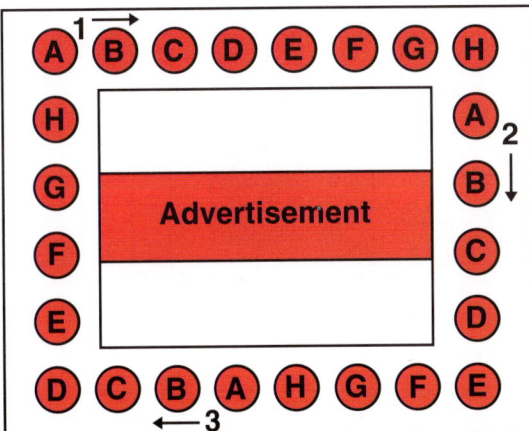

IC2 is a very flexible counter. With a few changes to the surrounding circuitry, it'll blink three diodes in a ring just as well as the eight shown. If we were to use this chip to power just three LEDs but did it by just leaving off the last five we'd soon notice that all wasn't as it should be. After the third LED turned off, there would be a pause while the chip finished counting up to eight. Pin 15 is the reset. If we were to connect the first unoccupied pin in the rotation (the pin 7, in this three LED example) to pin 15, the LEDs would "chase" uninterupted.

If you've studied the schematic closely you may wonder if the pin 9 (now connected to the reset input) could be used for a ninth LED. No problem. Connect the previously unused pin 11 to the reset input instead of pin 9.

If you want to build the 24 LED version see the additional schematic. The additional components are connected to points A-H.

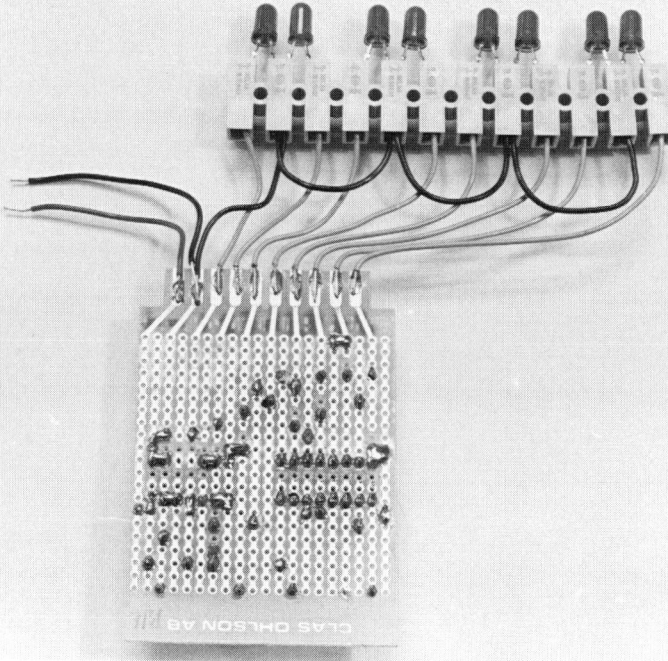

Miniguide
Bistable circuit using two monostable relays

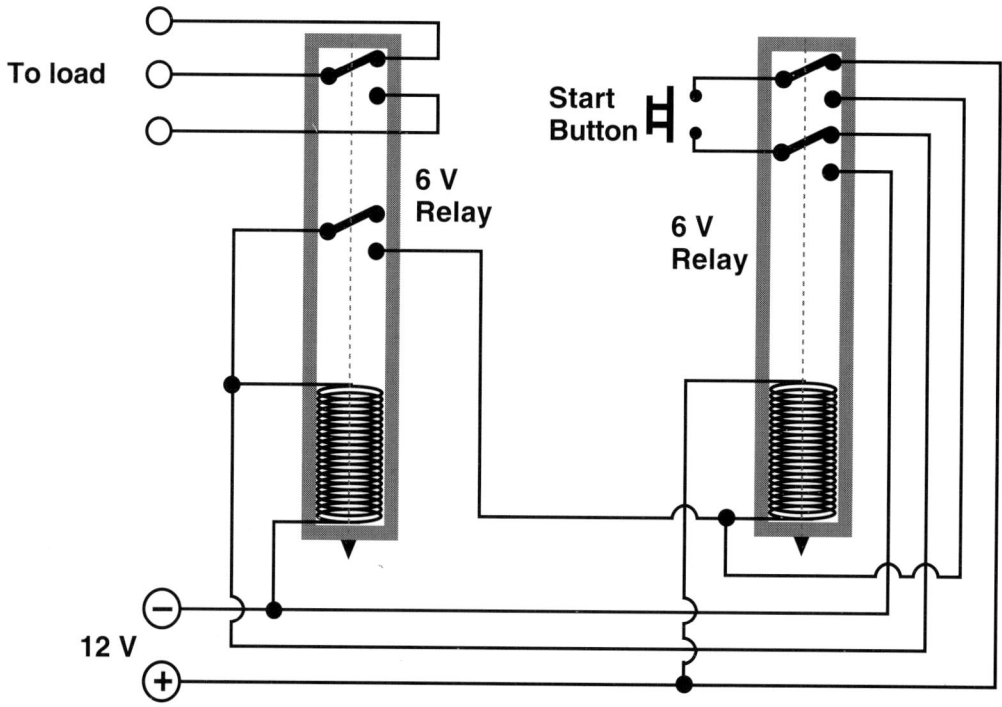

To load

Start
Button

6 V
Relay

6 V
Relay

12 V

IC2 is (a transistor and two resistors at each output) designed for powering a maximum of nine LEDs directly. Over that limit the extra current is too much for the chip.

The 24 LED version calls for a total of eight transistors, 16 resistors and 16 additional LEDs.

You may have noticed that the eight LED version doesn't call for current reducing resistors for the LEDs. That's because IC2 is designed for driving LEDs directly.

CONSTRUCTION

Despite the fact that we are working with just four active components I strongly recommend using a circuit board. These centipede like ICs are easy enough as it is to connect improperly. Pin numbering is given in the section on component descriptions. The module is dominated by the 15 short wires. The total of short wires on your module will vary depending upon if you want your leads arranged in numerical order. In that I have altered the circuit board by cutting through a portion of the copper strips, a photo showing the underside of the module is included as a construction aid.

IC sockets will spare you the anxiety of soldering directly to the ICs. The socket is soldered in place prior to inserting the IC. If you do need to replace the IC, replacement is greatly simplified.

CONNECTIONS

On my demo I have connected my LEDs to a terminal strip. How you mount yours will be determined by how you plan to use them. Use a ready made strip, fabricate your own from a piece of PC board with 10 stripes, separate leads – whatever works best. You can simplify the wiring by using common ground leads.

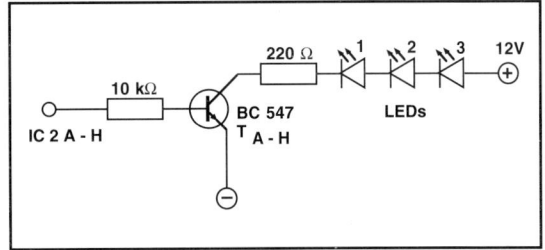

TROUBLESHOOTING

First of all, give the trimmer a turn. It may be turned down so low that the timer can't start. If that doesn't help, see the troubleshooting section of the previous chapter.

A logic probe is an excellent aid in tracing down faults on a circuit like this. It reads "1" and "0" (plus and minus). We'll be building a logic probe in a later chapter. A multimeter set on the DC mode will also work well.

VARIATIONS

The accompanying chart shows how to mount the 24 LED version in a frame application. The letters correspond to the letters on the schematic. As shown, the LEDs will chase in a clockwise direction. For a counter clockwise chase, just reverse the order.

Components	USA	UK
1 capacitor 0.22 µF	272-1070	1 JLØ1B
1 variable resistor 1 MΩ	271-211	1 UHØ9K
1 IC 4093 CMOS	276-2493	1 QW53H
1 IC 4017 CMOS	276-2417	1 QX09K
1 experimental perfboard	276-1395	1 JP47B
1 card-edge-connector	276-1564	1 FL86T
8 LEDs red 5 mm	276-044	8 UK48C
1 12-way block terminal	274-679	1 FE78K

Diesel horn

An earlier chapter covered steam locomotive whistles. Perhaps you don´t run steam but rather diesel or electric prototype locomotives. The whistle in this chapter is much more suitable for these types of locomotives.

As on the steam whistle project, you'll have to decide whether you'll be mounting this sound circuit on-board your locos or hidden in the layout scenery. I'll be giving you pointers for both applications.

The layout version has the advantage of a larger speaker (and better sound) and its on/off switch is a push-button switch, so mount the magnet aside of track. It's also easier to construct. The advantage of the on-board mount is that the sound is directional.

HOW IT WORKS
This circuit is nearly identical to the steam

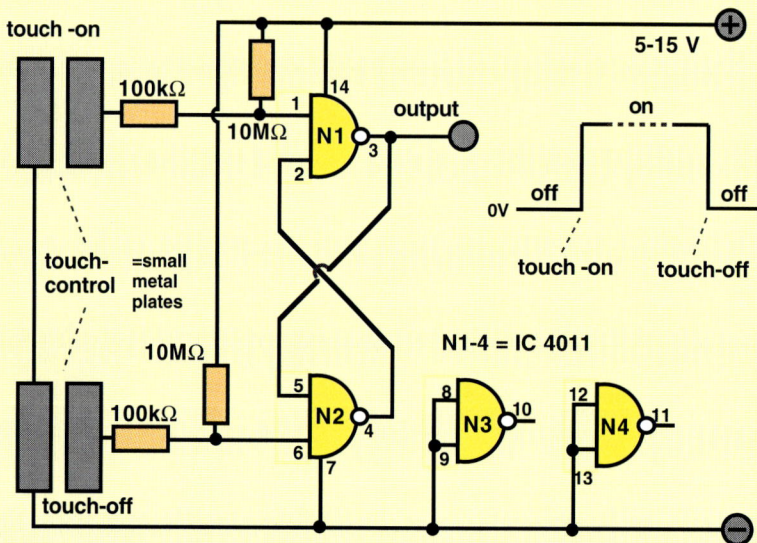

Miniguide
Touch control with memory (bistable)

touch -on

100kΩ
10MΩ N1
output
5-15 V
on
off
0V
off
off
touch -on
touch-off

touch-control = small metal plates

10MΩ
100kΩ

N1-4 = IC 4011

N2
N3
N4

touch-off

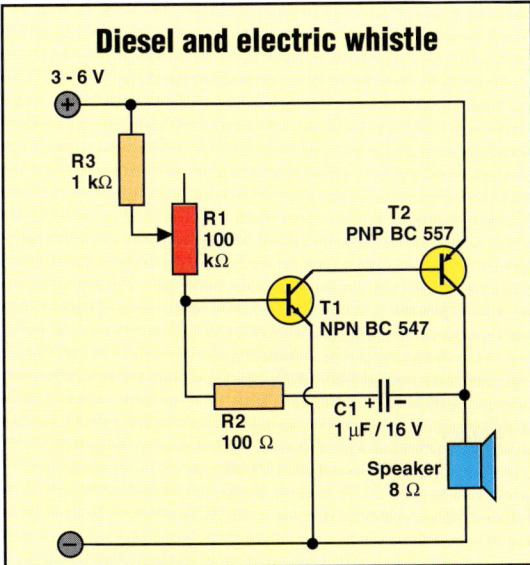

Diesel and electric whistle

3 - 6 V

R3 1 kΩ

R1 100 kΩ

T2 PNP BC 557

T1 NPN BC 547

R2 100 Ω

C1 1 μF / 16 V

Speaker 8 Ω

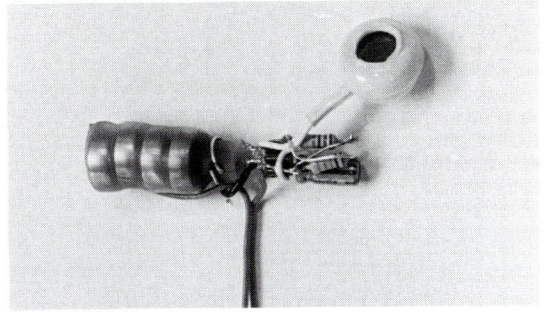

The photo shows a small electronic "clump". This clump is the compact version of this sound unit. Electronically, it`s nearly the same as its big brother. It´ll fit in an N scale locomotive with ease and I wouldn´t be surprised if it could be used in Z scale too – without using a shoehorn.

whistle. To lower the frequency, we'll be lowering the input voltage and using a capacitor of a higher value (one that takes longer to charge).

The trimpotentiometer adjusts the tone.

CONSTRUCTION

The photo shows the layout version. One of the outer legs of the trimmer is not used. Either bend it out of the way or solder it in place for added stability. Do not connect this leg electrically.

Construction of the on-board version will take a lot of careful planning and assembling. Unless your engines are larger than the norm, you can forget PC boards for this project. Solder the components directly to each other. If you're lucky, you'll have one,

sufficiently large, empty space in your engine. Most likely you'll have to divide the module into a series of sub-assemblies, making use of the space available to fit everything in. Three to four penlight batteries are an appropriate power source. Do not solder directly to the batteries. A battery holder is preferred but lacking space a substitution can be fabricated. Wrap the module or sub-modules in electricians tape to avoid shorts.

If you can't quite fit the unit into your engine consider mounting it in a freight or passenger car.

The onboard version is activated by a combination of reed switches and magnets. The reed switches are mounted either under the locomotive or on its sideframe. The activating magnets are glued in place along the right-of-way (either between the rails or slightly off to the side–whichever corresponds to reed switches). If you use Kadee couplers use the sideframe variation to avoid unwanted whistling.

Components	USA	UK
1 loudspeaker 8 Ω	40-245	1 YT25C
1 variable resistor 100 kΩ	271-284	1 UHØ6G
1 resistor 100Ω/0.25W	271-1311	1 M100Ω
1 resistor 10kΩ/0.25W	271-1335	1 M10kΩ
1 capacitor 1 μF/16V	272-1434	1 YY31J
1 transistor BC547	276-2009	1 QQ14Q
1 transistor BC 557	276-2023	1 QQ16S
1 magnetic earpiece 8 Ω	20-210	1 LB23A
1 experimental perfboard	276-1395	1 JP47B
1 card-edge-connector	276-1564	1 FL86T

Voltage tester

As opposed to the instrument we constructed in an earlier chapter, this one is a precision intrument. We can adjust it to indicate when a DC voltage has fallen below a predetermined level. A too low voltage will give a red indication. If all is well, it will show green.

HOW IT WORKS

This circuit is built around an IC 555. The trimmer determines the voltage at which the instrument will show red. As long as the measured voltage is up to the predetermined value, the green LED will light. If the voltage is less than it should be, the red LED will light for two seconds. If the voltage drop was just temporary (under two seconds),

the red LED will turn off and the green LED will light after the two seconds are up. If the voltage drop was not temporary, the red LED will continue to shine.

You may wish to use the instrument to indicate voltages that are too high instead. Just switch the green and red LEDs.

CONSTRUCTION

The intended use for this instrument should determine how it is constructed. In that it is a universal instrument it can be utilized in other areas besides model railroading. It could be used, for example, to check that a car battery is fully charged. The module can be built to fit in a small enclosure together with its power source, a nine volt battery.

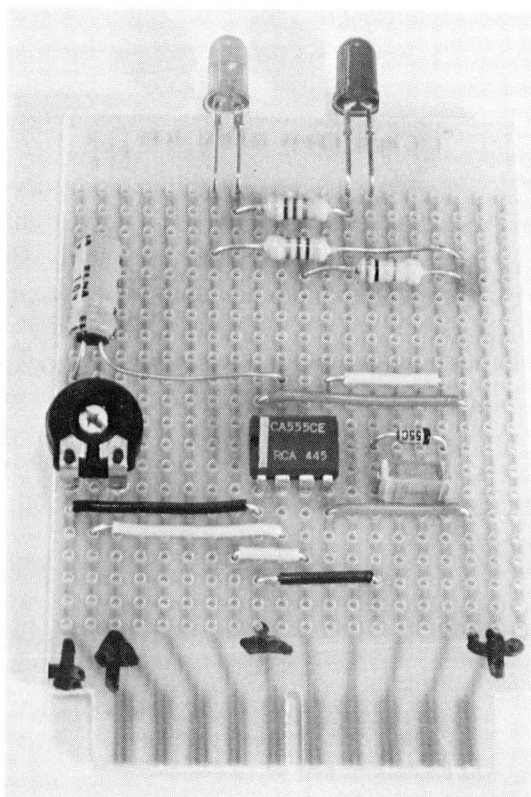

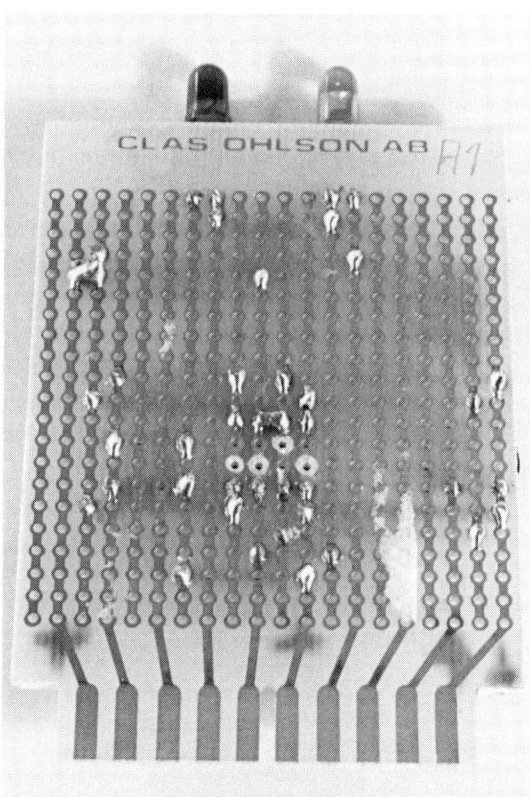

Voltage tester

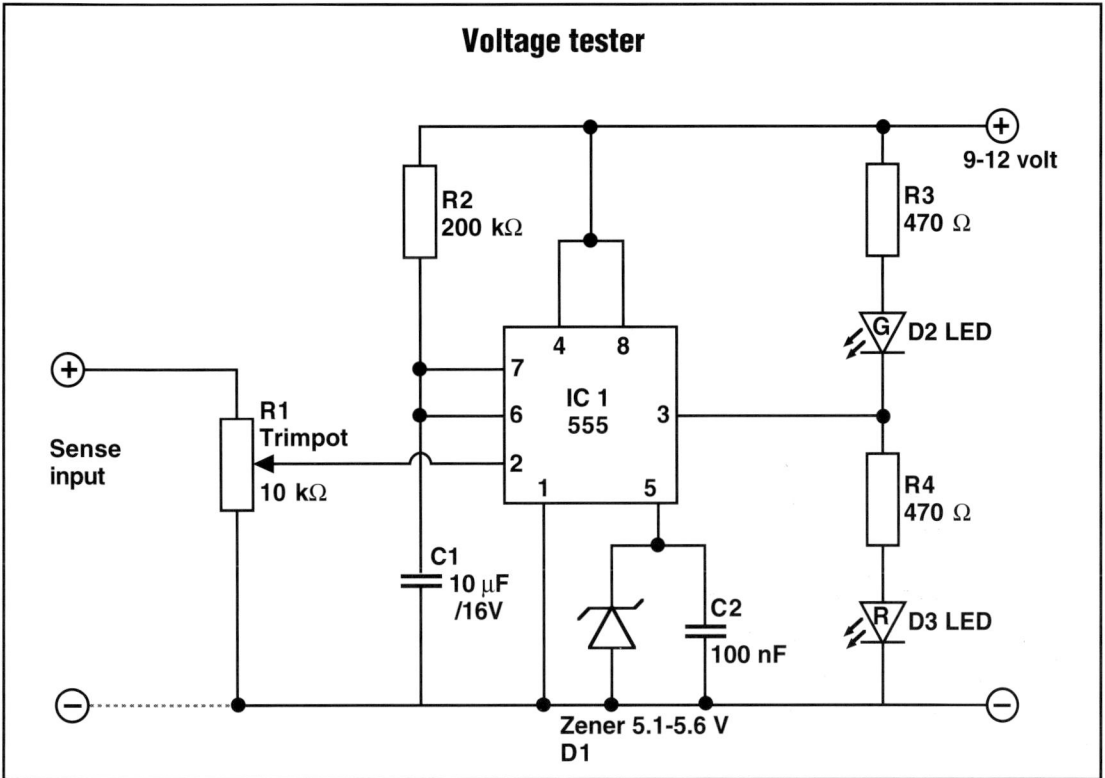

Substitute the trimpotentiometer for a potentiometer and mount it in the enclosure to conveniently vary the measuring scale from between 4.5 and 16 volts.

The components have plenty of space. The layout is shown in the photo. Only four breaks in the circuit board's copper strips were necessary. All were between the IC pins. A "solder pearl" was used to bridge the gap between two strips.

CALIBRATION

You'll need a voltmeter or multimeter for calibration and a variable DC power source.

Connect both the voltmeter and DC power source to the instrument's test leads. Adjust the voltage to the desired setting.

Using a small screwdriver turn the trimmer until the tester shifts from red to green, Test your setting by varying the DC. You'll probably need to do a little fine tuning.

Components	USA	UK
1 IC timer 555	276-1723	1 QH66W
1 resistor 200kΩ/0.25W	2x271-1311	1 M200kΩ
1 resistor 470kΩ/0.25W	271-1354	1 M470kΩ
1LED red 5 mm	276-044	1 UK48C
1LED green 5 mm	276-022	1 UK49D
1 trimpotentiometer 10 kΩ	271-282	1 UH03D
1 capacitor 10 µF/16V	272-1025	1 JL05F
1 capacitor 0.1 µF	272-135	1 WW41U
1 zenerdiode 5.1-5.6V*	276-565	1 QF46A
1 experimental perfboard	276-1395	1 JP47B
1 card-edge-connector	276-1564	1 FL86T
*Jameco order No.		

Logic probe

Modern electronics have revolutioned test equipment. Small signals, interference sensivity, short pulses and extremely compact construction are common to IC technology. All too often the old reliable multimeter just won't do the job.

The logic probe is a special instrument designed for IC technology and it is invaluable in troubleshooting and fine tuning. Probes are available commercially for $50 and upwards. We'll be building our own for under one dollar.

As opposed to the other instrument projects in this book, the logic probe isn't suitable for general layout use. It's meant for measuring the low voltages and pulses of IC chips.

If we were to measure a connection in a circuit to determine if it was grounded or not, a voltmeter could easily mislead us. While a voltmeter would give a reading of 0 volts for a ground, it would give the same reading for a connection that was not connected at all. The logic probe will give readings that differentiate between the two.

A voltmeter can create faults where none existed before. Connecting a voltmeter to a IC can cause interference problems. The logic probe will not interfere with the internal workings of IC chips.

A voltmeter would be useless for measuring all but the lowest of frequencies. The probe uses a green LED to indicate "1" (full voltage) and a red LED to indicate "0" (no voltage). If the incoming or outgoing signal pulses are too quick for the red and green indicators a third, yellow LED will light.

HOW IT WORKS
IC 40106 contains six Schmitt trigger circuits. They can be used separately or together.

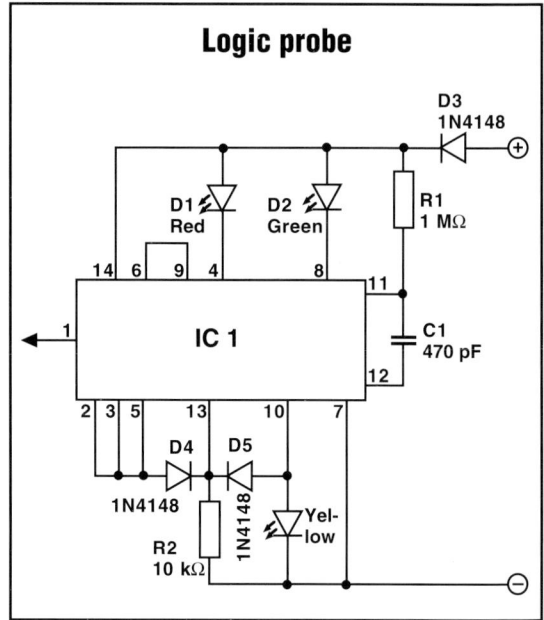

Logic probe

The IC is a CMOS type. CMOS chips can be powered by any voltage in the 3 to 15 volt range. This makes the circuit especially well suited for use in a probe. The logic probe will work just as well on either 5 volt or 12 volt circuits.

Each of the six internal circuits of IC40106 is an inverter. That means that if you put in a plus you'll get a minus out and vice versa.

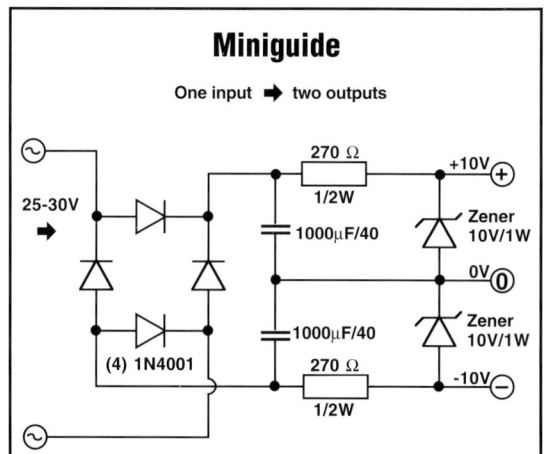

Miniguide

One input ➡ two outputs

a large felt pen casing instead. The main consideration is that the completed probe will be small enough for use in tight quarters.

If you decide to build the test probe on a large circuit board and use leads to make your measurements, either put the circuitry in a casing or wrap it with electricians tape. Touching the components with your hand will give false readings.

HOW TO USE IT

The probe needs a power source to work. Two of the three leads are power leads. Always connect these to the plus and minus of the circuit to be tested. The advantage of using circuit's own power is that the probe "knows" where the threshold is between "1" and "0".

The probe is equipped with a diode at its plus power input that will protect the unit from damage should the power leads be connected improperly.

You should get both a red and a green indication when you connect the power leads. A green at a test point indicates "1". and red "0". Red plus green means the test point is unconnected. Pulses of ones and zeros will alternately light the green and red LEDs. High frequency pulses will also light the yellow IC. The probe will measure frequencies up to 1 megahertz.

More elaborate probes are available but for model railroad circuits, this logic probe is more than adequete.

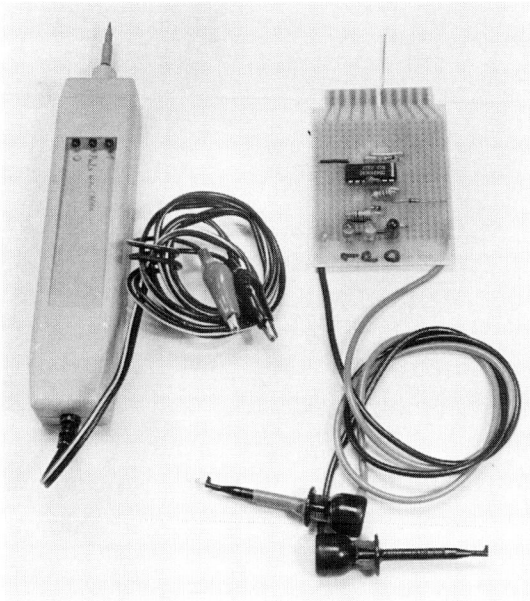

Four of the inverters are used to turn the red and green LEDs off and on. The other two are used for the pulse memory function.

A Schmitt trigger has a hairline definition of what a "1" or "0" is. Even if the input voltage is increased gradually, the trigger won't switch from "1" to "0" until the input voltage reaches a predetermined threshold.

CONSTRUCTION

Ideally, the circuit should be built in one small, compact unit. The photo shows a commercial probe casing. They come complete with test tips and leads. If you like, use

Components	USA	UK
3 diodes 1N4148	276-1122	3 QL80B
3 LEDs red 5 mm	276-044	3 UK48C
1 IC 40106 CMOS *	CD40106	1 QW64U
1 resistor 10kΩ/0.25W	271-1335	1 M10kΩ
1 resistor 1MΩ/0.25W	271-1356	1 M1MΩ
1 capacitor 470 pF	272-125	1 WX64U
1 experimental perfboard	276-1395	1 JP47B
1 card-edge-connector	276-1564	1 FL86T
2 test clips	270-372	2 FM37S
*Jameco order No.		

Crosswalk warning lights

Most layout signalling is used to regulate railroad operations. In this chapter we'll be building a signal for Main Street.

Normally, the trains are the movers on our layouts. Auto traffic is always at a standstill – not much activity with the wee folk either. If we're going to start up those warning lights we'll need a system that will run itself.

The circuit is based on European prototype warning lights. The explanation of the circuitry will give you the knowledge to adapt the circuit to your own needs.

I've used an oscillator IC that activates the signal periodically. You'll decide how often by the surrounding components you select.

The IC is a 555 that will give us the desired results with very few additional components and it isn't as sensitve for static electricity as the CMOS ICs.

HOW IT WORKS

In this circuit we'll be using IC555 as a multivibrator with a bistable function. It swings at a low frequency between two positions. How fast or slow is determined by our choice of components and the adjustment at the trimmer.

The schematic shows the 555 as a box. We'll be using all of the pins with the

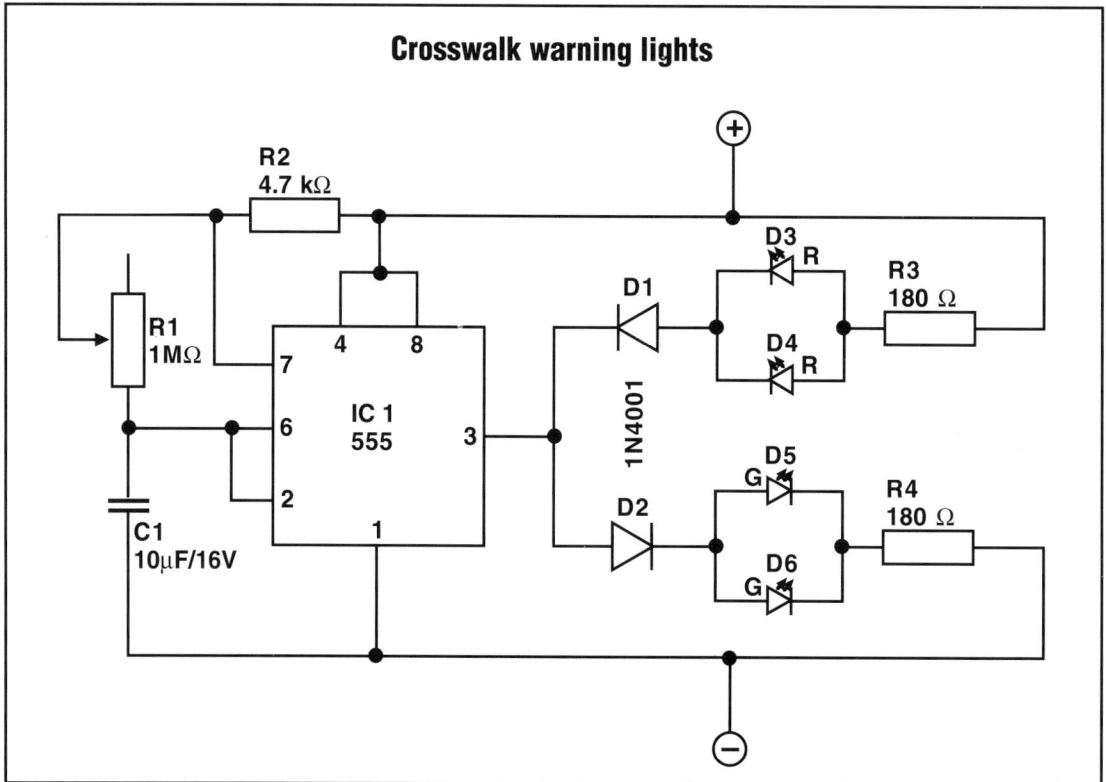

Crosswalk warning lights

The schematic shows parallel connected LEDs. This often simplifies wiring. If it is important that they shine with exactly the same light intensity, connect them in series. The same current will then pass through both LEDs.

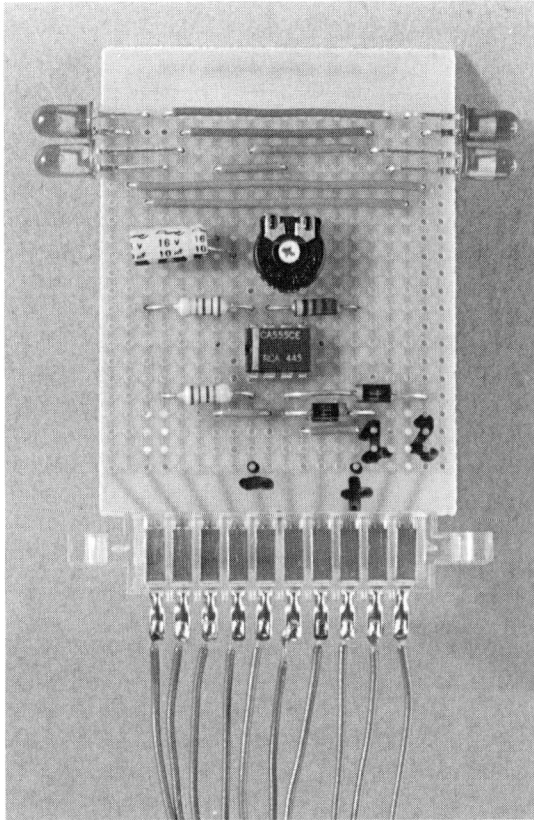

exception of pin 5. The resistors and capacitors to the left of the IC determine the frequency. The components to the right make up the light portion of the circuit. With the trimmer we can adjust the frequency so that pin 3 switches from between "1" and "0" at different speeds. Pin 3 can be compared with a relay. When pin 3 is high ("1"), it's the same as a relay's closed contact connected to plus. When pin 3 is low ("0"), it's grounded.

I have connected my module to a 12 volt power source. That means that pin 3 switches between two stable conditions – ground and 12 volts. The circuit can be powered by any voltage in the 5 to 12 volt range.

If we take a closer look at the light portion of the circuit we'll see that there are four LEDs. They are divided between two sub-circuits. The red LEDs are connected between plus and pin 3. When pin 3 is low a current flows through the red LEDs.

The other sub-circuit is connected between pin 3 and minus. When pin 3 is high, the green LEDs light. D1 blocks the red sub-circuit when pin 3 is high.

CONSTRUCTION

Besides the LEDs, this projects requires eight components and that means that we´ll be needing a circuit board. In practice, they are to be mounted on signal masts.

I began construction by placing the components on the circuit board to check that everything would fit. The 555 was soldered in place and the copper strips between the opposing pins were cut. Without these cuts, for example, pins 1 and 8 would have been connected to each other. In that pin 1 is ground and pin 8 is plus, a short circuit would have been a certainty.

The next component was the trim-potentiometer. It was connected between pins 6 and 7 with its third terminal at pin 5. The copper strip was cut at pin 5. With the layout I used, no other cuts were required.

Looking at the photo you may think that I missed a connection at the capacitor´s minus leg. From the component side it looks as if it is unconnected. But in that its copper strip is a "neighbor" to the IC´s pin 1, I have intentionally connected these two together on the underside with a solder pearl. You could, of course, replace the pearl with a short piece of wire.

The photo shows my module. The best component placement will depend on the design of your printed circuit board.

Finally, note that if the two LEDs are not connected to pin 3 but only to each other, they would form a circuit between 12 volts and ground. This would cause both the red and green LEDs to light at the same time.

ADJUSTMENTS

With the components shown, the signal

will operate in five to ten second cycles. Switch to a 1 µF capacitor and your cycles will be in the one to four seconds range. A 100 µF capacitor will push the range over a minute.

CONNECTIONS

My module requires just two plus leads. Signal mast-mounted LEDs require four more leads (two to each LED pair). Another variation calls for moving even more components off the circuit board (the diodes and LED resistors). By doing this one can locally connect the LED sub-circuits to plus and minus. Only one lead would be required to the circuit board and IC pin 3. What is best will vary from application to application.

Components	USA	UK
1 timer IC 555	276-1723	1 QH66W
1 resistor 4.7kΩ/0.25W	271-1330	1 M4.7kΩ
2 resistors 180Ω/0.25W	271-1110	2 M180Ω
1 variable resistor 1MΩ	271-211	1 UHØ9k
1 capacitor 10 µF/16V	272-1025	1 JLØ5F
2 diodes 1N4001	276-1101	2 QL73Q
2 LEDs red 5 mm	276-044	2 UK48C
2 LEDs green 5 mm	276-022	2 UK49D
1 experimental perfboard	276-1395	1 JP47B
1 card-edge-connector	276-1564	1 FL86T

Miniguide – Train Indicator

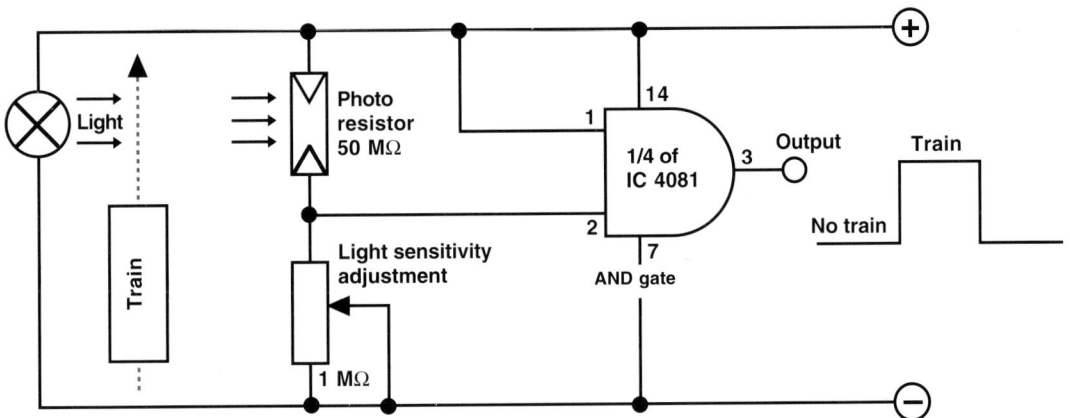

Light

Photo resistor 50 MΩ

Train

Light sensitivity adjustment

1 MΩ

14

1

2

7

1/4 of IC 4081

AND gate

3

Output

Train

No train

Miniguide – Frequency doubler

Pulse input left side = F(Hz) generates 2F(Hz) at output (right).

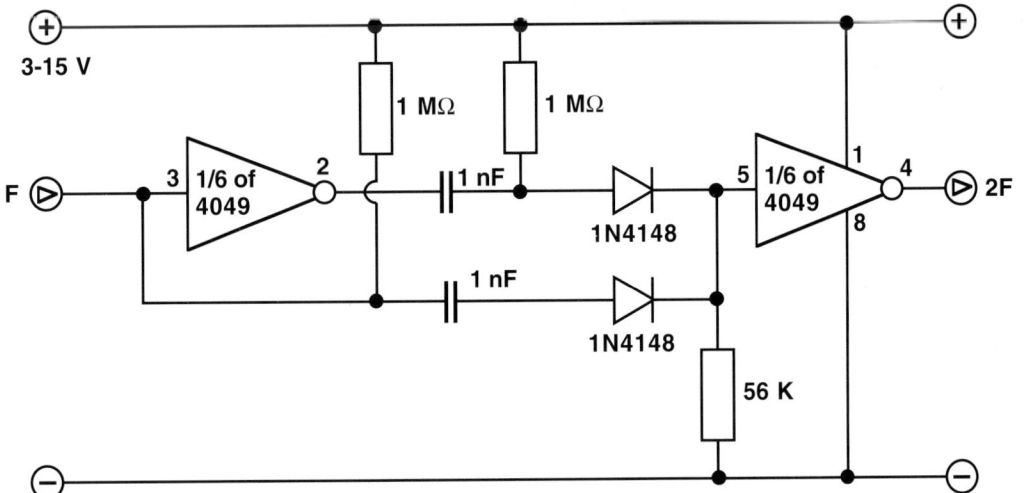

3-15 V

F

3

2

1/6 of 4049

1 MΩ

1 MΩ

1 nF

1N4148

1 nF

1N4148

56 K

5

1

4

8

1/6 of 4049

2F

Note! IC pins 7, 9, 11 and 14 must be grounded if unused

55

European style police siren

As opposed to the other sound circuits in this book, this one isn't meant for train use. This siren can be used for police cars, fire engines and ambulances.

With a little ingenuity you should even be able to use it in N scale vehicles.

We'll be using an almost classic circuit that uses two oscillators, working in combination to produce a two-tone siren exactly as that used on European emergency vehicles. It has also been used in recent years in the US as a complement to the common, wailing siren.

To save space, we'll be using a CMOS 4011. It contains four NAND gates. These gates and a few surrounding resistors and capacitors make up the two oscillators.

HOW IT WORKS

To vary the frequence for a so realistic sound as possible, the circuit has a trim potentiometer. If you need to fit the module into a N scale vehicle substitute the trimmer for a 270 to 330 kΩ resistor. The tone will also be effected by your choice of input voltage.

My demo module was originally powered by four 1.5 penlight batteries. I later increased the voltage to 9 volts and switched the capacitor between pins 9 and 11 from 100 nF to 20 µF. The tone was much better after the changes.

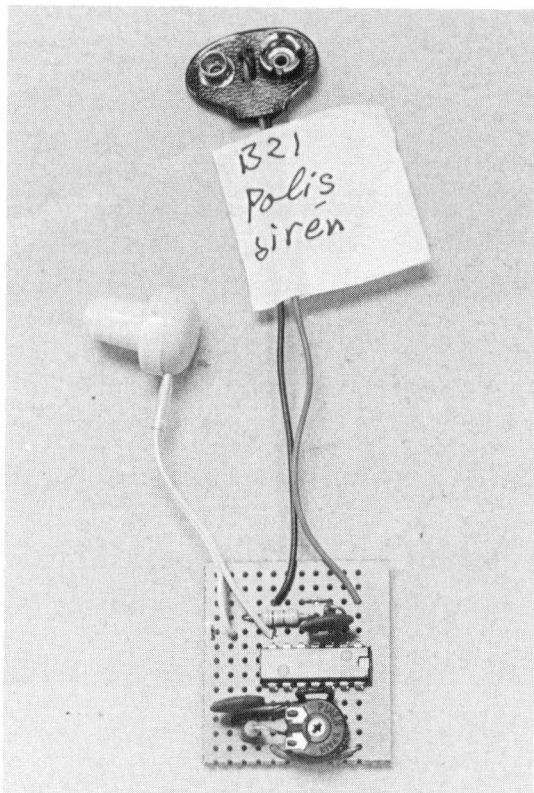

I used an earphone as a speaker. The casing can be carefully trimmed down to both reduce its size and increase the volume.

In H0 and larger scales a small amplifier and real speakers can be used. IC TDA 2003 is a complete amplifier. It's short circuit proof, has an output of 10 watts and your train room will sound like a major crime scene.

Components	USA	UK
1 variable resistor 1 MΩ	271-211	1 UHØ9K
1 resistor 4.7MΩ	2x271-1135	1 M4.7MΩ
1 resistor 470 kΩ	271-1354	1 M470 kΩ
1 resistor 2.2 MΩ	1x271-1135	1 M2.2MΩ
1 CMOS IC 4011	276-2411	1 QX05F
2 capacitors 0.1 µF	272-135	2 YR75S
1 magnetic earpiece 8Ω	20-210	1 LB23A
1 experimental perfboard	276-1395	1 JP47B

Miniguide

3V (2 penlight batteries)

Switch

12 | N1 | 11 | 8 | N2 | 10

13

LED   1N4148

1 | N3 | 3 | 4 | N4 | 6

2 | | | 5

N1-4 = 1 X 4001 IC

R = 100 kΩ

To switch pluses

CONSTRUCTION

To reduce space requirements you can use the IC as a base for the module. Solder the components directly to the chip. Beginners can use an IC socket. When the soldering work is completed, just plug in the IC. As long as you use an earphone as a speaker you can use miniature batteries as a power source. Fullsize batteries can be mounted under the layout and connected to the modules via power leads.

European style siren

4.5-9 V

C1 | 100 nF

R1
470 K

R2
2.2
MΩ

Earphone

IC 1   4011

14 | 13 | 12 | 11 | 10 | 9 | 8

1 | 2 | 3 | 4 | 5 | 6 | 7

R4
4.7
MΩ

R3
470 kΩ

C2
100
nF

Directional locomotive lighting

In the next chapters we'll be taking a closer look at locomotive and car illumination for both DC and AC operations.

In this chapter we'll be building a simple headlight module that lights the appropriate headlight or headlights depending on the train's direction of travel.

As far as headlights go, we can divide all model railroad locomotives into three classes. The least expensive have no functioning headlights at all. A step up and you get headlights that light in at least one direction but only light when the engine is moving. Top of the line locos usually have it all-directional, constant lighting, often switching from clear to red when the engine is reversed.

If you only have top of the line motive power, this chapter isn't for you. We'll be concentrating on improvements for the low and middle classes of locomotives.

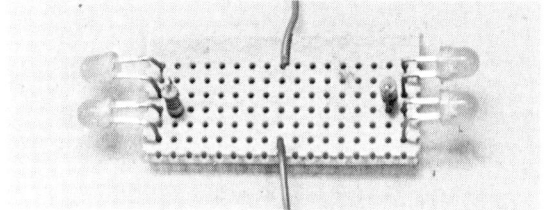

HOW IT WORKS

Model locomotives are nearly always equipped with miniature lamps. Lamps are expensive and have a relatively limited lifetime. A LED, in comparison, is inexpensive and will last for years. Recently, LEDs have been developed that produce much more light than the older versions.

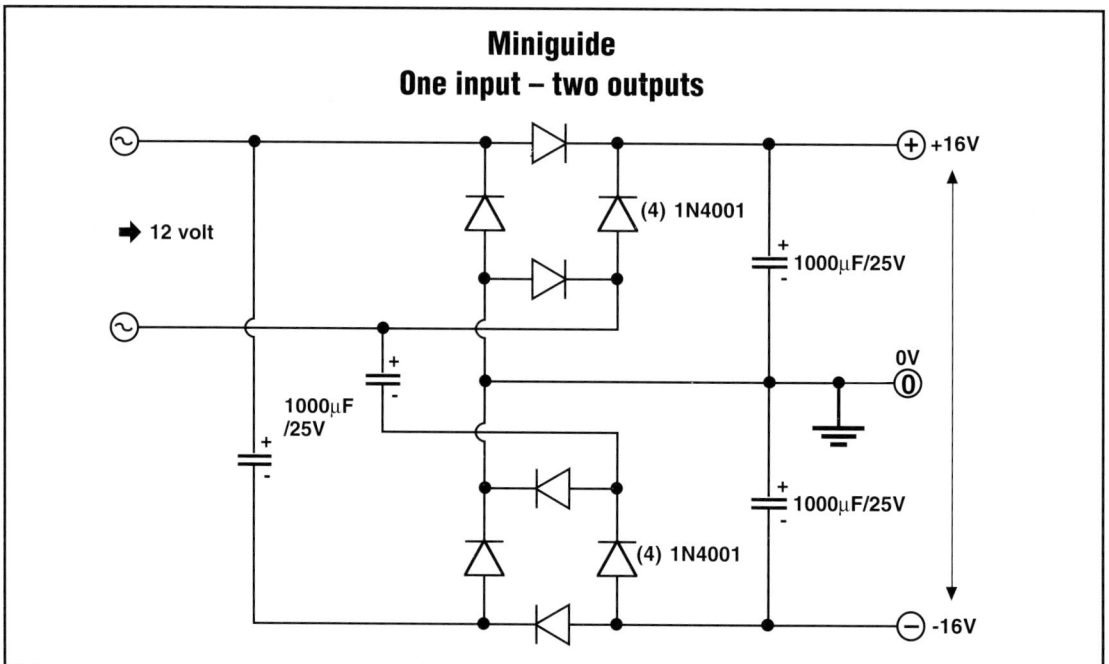

Miniguide
One input – two outputs

12 volt

(4) 1N4001

1000μF/25V

1000μF/25V

1000μF/25V

+16V

0V

-16V

If your locomotives are equipped with lamps, use them and their accompanying leads. You'll only need to connect a diode in series with each headlight. For dual end headlights connect the diodes so that only one end at a time gets power. In that there is a 50 percent chance that the wrong headlight will light, test the loco before replacing the shell. If the wrong headlight turns on, just reverse the diodes.

If your locos have no lamps, you can just as well use LEDs. The schematic shows a directional circuit in a double headlight application. In this circuit the LEDs work as both light sources and diodes and no other diodes are required.

The circuit's 680Ω resistors are suitable for H0 and N scales' maximum track power of 14 to 16 volts. For Z scale substitute them for 330Ω resistors.

CONSTRUCTION

In the smaller scales, you'll probably have to construct this circuit without a circuit board. Drill holes in the locomotive's ends and glue the LEDs in place. When the glue has set, solder the resistors in place. Model locomotives often have one motor pole connected to the chassis. Locate a suitable connection point for the headlight circuit.

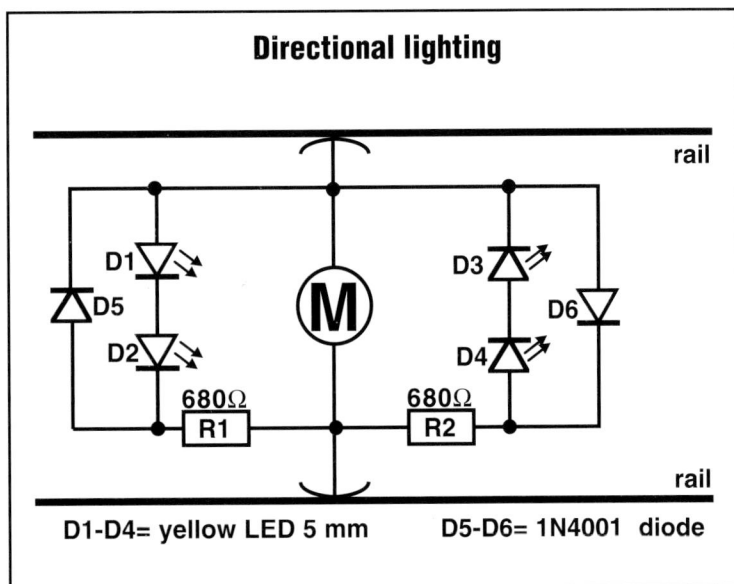

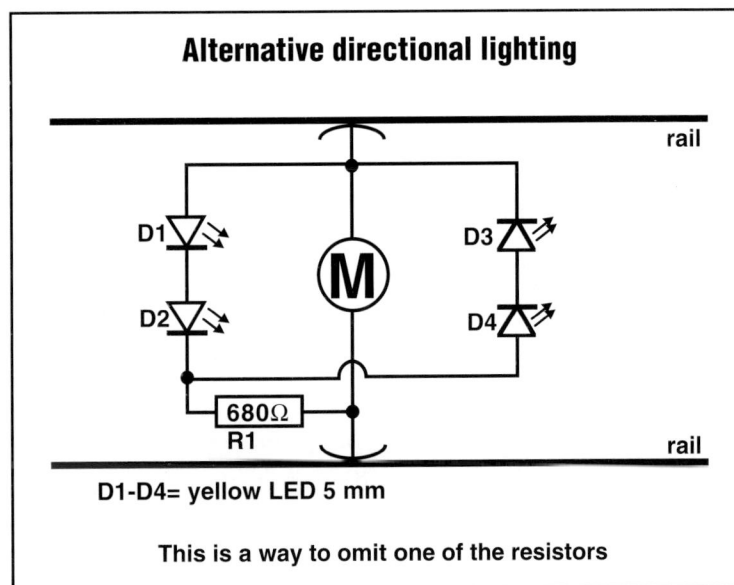

Directional lighting

D1-D4= yellow LED 5 mm   D5-D6= 1N4001 diode

Alternative directional lighting

D1-D4= yellow LED 5 mm

This is a way to omit one of the resistors

Components	USA	UK
2 resistor 680Ω/0.25W	271-1117	2 M680R
4 LED yellow 5 mm	276-021	4 UK50E
1 experimental perfboard	276-1395	1 JP47B

Constant locomotive lighting

This circuit will give us a constant level of light from our locomotives' headlights, regardless of train speed.

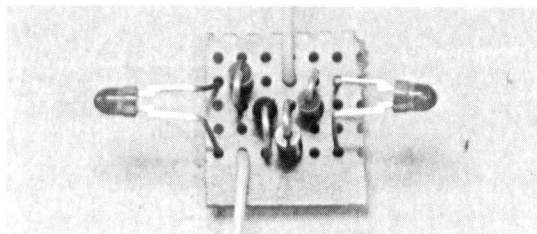

Select another circuit if you use a pulse controller.

Even model locos in the higher price ranges are often lacking one important feature. The headlights won't light when they are standing still. At slow speeds the headlights give off a soft glow. Not until they're running at bullet train speeds do the headlights shine at full strength. With six components, we can correct this fault.

HOW IT WORKS

We'll be taking advantage of the fact that model locomotive motors do not start their rotation below 1.3 volts. Usually 3 volts are required to overcome an H0 engine's friction resistance. This circuit will turn the headlights on before the engine's motor begins to rotate.

The second "electronic law" we'll be taking advantage of deals with diode voltage drops. The voltage drop over a diode is .6 to .7 volts.

If we connect two diodes in series we'll get a voltage drop of about 1.3 volts. This is exactly the voltage requirement to light a LED.

As you can see in the schematic, this circuit is made up of LEDs and diodes connected in series to a motor. This circuit will subtract .7 volts from the engine's top end speed. In that we rarely run at maximum speeds, this should not be a problem.

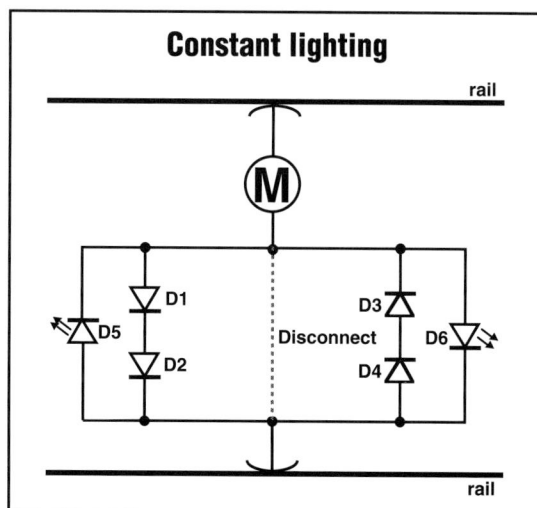

Constant lighting

The diodes' voltage drop is constant. Regardless of engine speed, the LEDs will shine at the same intensity throughout the track voltage range.

VARIATIONS

Combinations of 1.5 V lamps and LEDs can be used to suit various types of motive power. 1.5 volt lamps can be substituted for LEDs on any of these lighting circuits.

Components	USA	UK
2 LED red 5 mm	276-044	2 UK48C
4 diode 1N4001	276-1101	4 QL73Q
1 experimental perfboard	276-1395	1 JP47B

Constant lighting for AC locos

Most of the projects in this book can be used on either DC or AC layouts. The constant lighting circuits are exceptions. In this chapter we'll be building a module for use on AC powered model locomotives. This circuit is not suitable for DC locos. It is unnecessarily complex and doesn't activate the headlights until track voltage has reached 8 volts.

HOW IT WORKS

Track current enters the circuit at Rectifier D. The schematic shows the rectifier as four separate diodes. If you don't have diodes on hand use a full-wave bridge rectifier instead. It's less expensive than the four diodes and eases module construction.

From the rectifier, current is filtered by C1 and passes through R1 and R2. D1 is a zener diode. A zener diode is a modified version of a standard diode. Up to its rated voltage (in this case 3.9 V) it functions as a

common diode. Over 3.9 volts it passes only current which keeps the voltage to its rated level. R1 and R2 help limit current to both the LEDs and the zener diode. R3 is a final current limiter for the LEDs.

1 watt and 400 milliwatt are common zener diode values. This circuit uses the former. We have now reached a point where

Constant lighting for AC locomotives

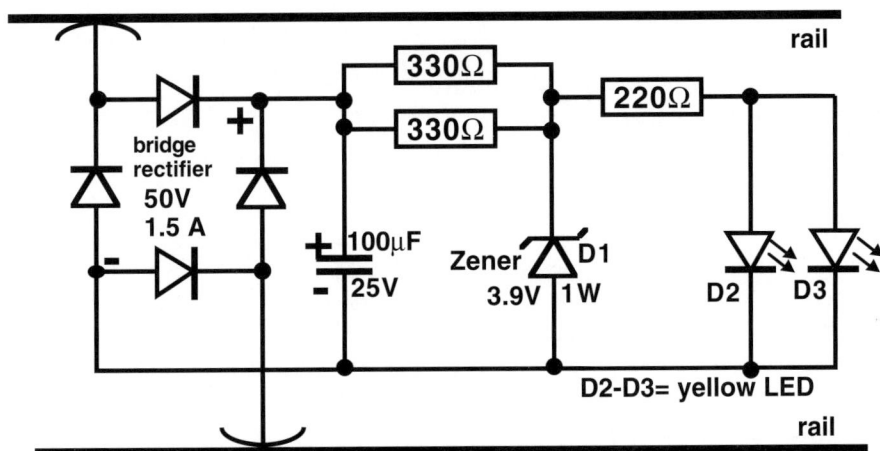

bridge rectifier 50V 1.5 A

330Ω
330Ω
220Ω

100µF 25V

Zener D1 3.9V 1W

D2   D3

D2-D3= yellow LED

rail

rail

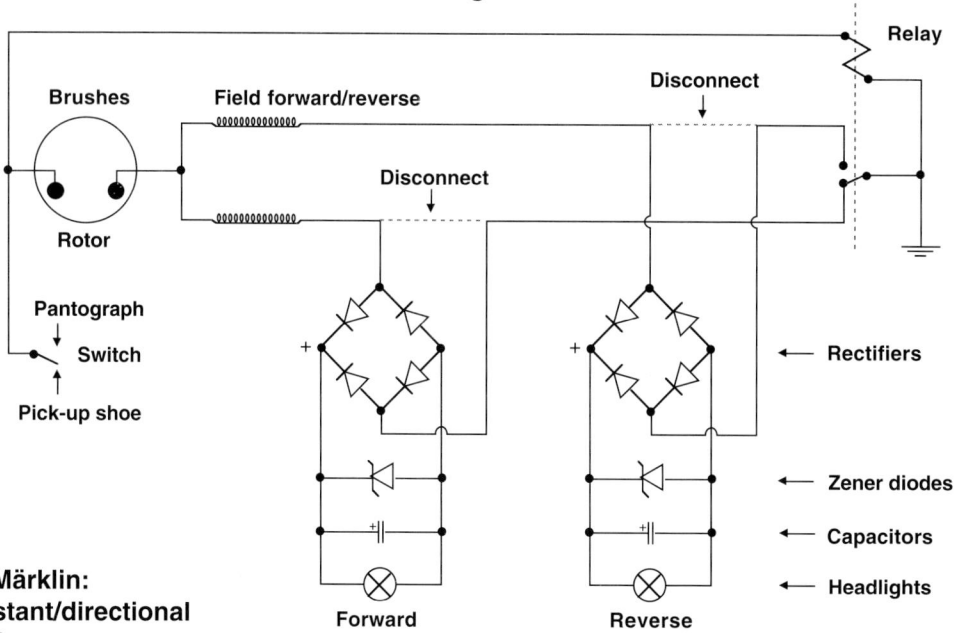

Miniguide

Brushes

Field forward/reverse

Disconnect

Relay

Rotor

Disconnect

Pantograph

Switch

Pick-up shoe

Rectifiers

Zener diodes

Capacitors

Headlights

For Märklin:
Constant/directional
lighting

Forward

Reverse

Note: 3V. lamps, 1N4001 diods, 3.3V. Zener diodes, 100µF/10V electrolytic capacitors

voltage is stable, regardless of track voltage variations. A current reducing resistor is connected in series with the LEDs.

AC locos are reversed by an onboard relay. This is activated by a voltage pulse from the transformer. Even while reversing, the engine's headlights will remain lit with almost unchanged intensity.

CONSTRUCTION

The photo shows the module on a single PC board. Space restrictions usually call for splitting the module between at least two separate boards. Be careful that the module is isolated from the loco-motive chassis.

CONNECTIONS

Connect one of the rectifier's AC terminals to the engine's chassis and the other to the common reverser lead.

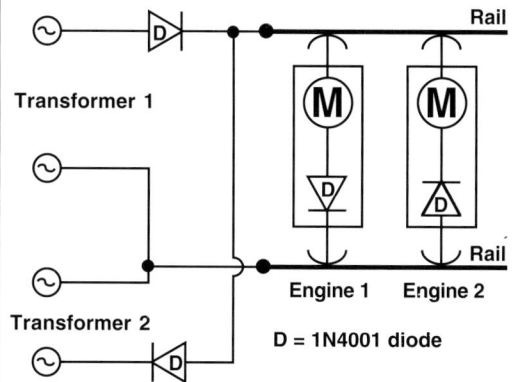

Miniguide – Two train running

Rail

Transformer 1

Transformer 2

Engine 1   Engine 2

D = 1N4001 diode

Components	USA	UK
2 LED yellow 5 mm	276-021	2 UK50E
1 resistor 220Ω/0.25W	271-1313	1 M220R
1 resistor 330Ω/0.25W	271-1315	1 M330R
1 capacitor 100µF/25V	272-1028	1 FB49D
1 bridge rectifier 50V/1.5A	276-1152	1 QL37S
2 zenerdiodes 3.9V/0.4W *	1N750	2 QHØ4E
1 experimental perfboard	276-1395	1 JP47B
* Jameco order no		

End-of-train warning lights

This circuit will give your trains' rear end protection and it'll do it even when they're standing still. While the schematic shows the double light system common in Europe, the circuit can be adapted to other prototypes.

As soon as track voltage has passed 2.5 volts (which is lower than the starting voltage of most model locomotives), the warning lights will light. Light intensity is constant from 3 to 16 volts.

You should be able to fit this six component module in all cars from N scale and upwards.

This circuit is directional (the lights go out when the train reverses).

If you'll be using this unit in a car equipped with interior lighting, just connect it in parallel to the existing lighting. Unlit cars call for rigging up some form of power pick-up. Commercial pick-ups are available.

HOW IT WORKS

The two small, signal transistors are the heart of this little current shunter. They insure that the LEDs current draw is limited to 22 to 35 Amps. Track voltage opens T1 and the LEDs light. T2 is activated by the current passing through T1. If T1 begins to open too much, T2 opens just enough to drop the voltage at T1's base and consequently restricts T1's current flow.

Only five components are used and all are small. They can be packed together on a small circuit board and fit in an N scale car.

Although the circuit was designed for end of train warning lights it would also work well for powering locomotive headlights. My demonstration module, shown in the photo, was constructed with yellow LEDs which are more suitable for headlight applications.

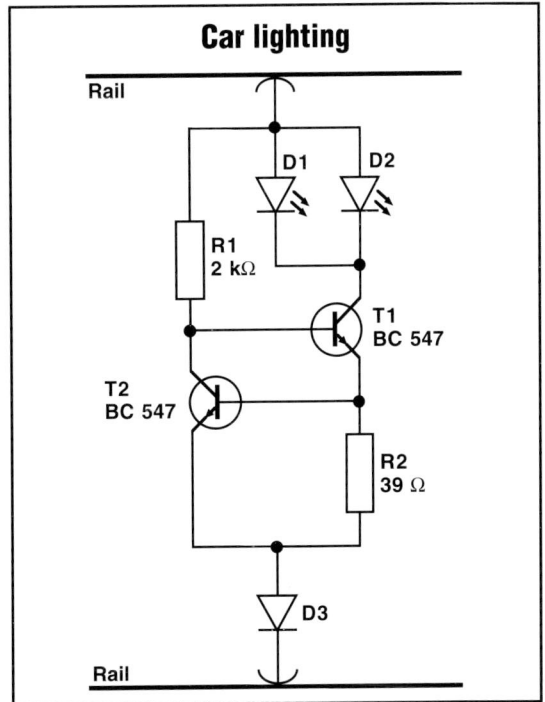

Car lighting

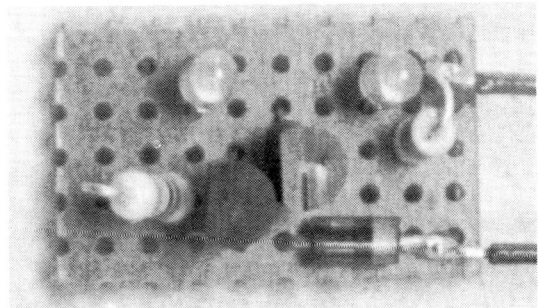

Components	USA	UK
2 LEDs red 5 mm	276-044	2 UK48C
2 transistors BC 547	276-2009	2 QQ14Q
1 resistor 2 kΩ/0.25W	271-1325	1 M2kΩ
1 resistor 39Ω/0.25W	271-1105	1 M39R
1 diode 1N4001	276-1101	1 QL73Q
1 experimental perfboard	276-1395	1 JP47B

Switch machine amplifier

Sooner or later you'll find that your transformer just doesn't have the current output to run your growing train layout. You'll notice it first on your switches. Operational reliability will drop. While some switches may continue to function properly, others will only work intermittently. This module will solve this problem and at a fraction of the cost of a new transformer.

A method of switching that has won a lot of ground among model railroaders these past years is matrix switching. Switches are not thrown one at a time. A route is chosen and all switches along that route are thrown at the same time by a push of a single button. In that the switches can be activated by a variety of route selections, a network of diodes is required to guide current to the proper points. Matrixes are used in both the chapter on traffic lights and the chapter on automatic drawbridge control.

Switches need a lot of current, but only momentarily. If several switches are to be

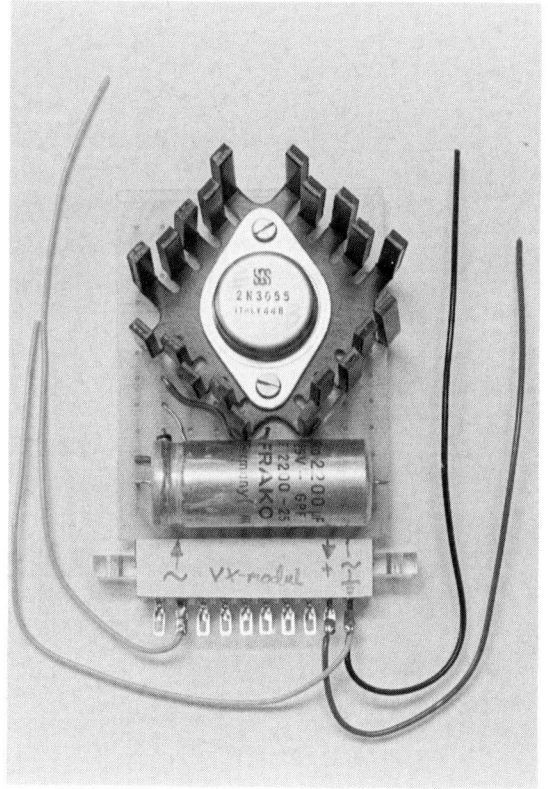

Switch machine amplifier – heavy duty version

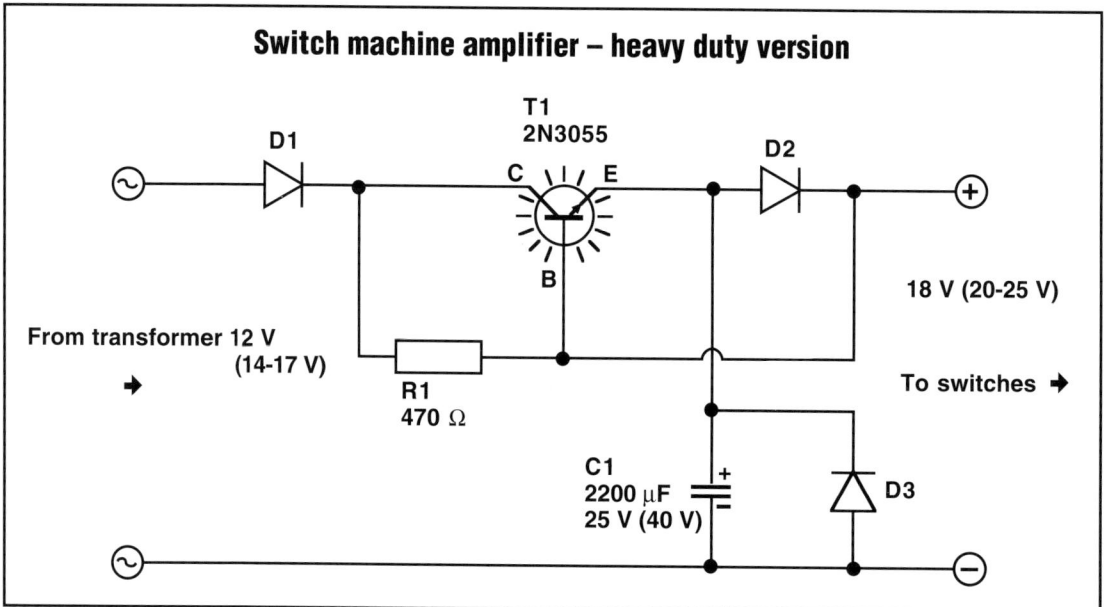

D1

T1
2N3055

C \|/ E
B

D2

From transformer 12 V
(14-17 V)

R1
470 Ω

18 V (20-25 V)

To switches ➜

C1
2200 μF
25 V (40 V)

D3

(+)

(−)

Switch machine amplifier – light duty version

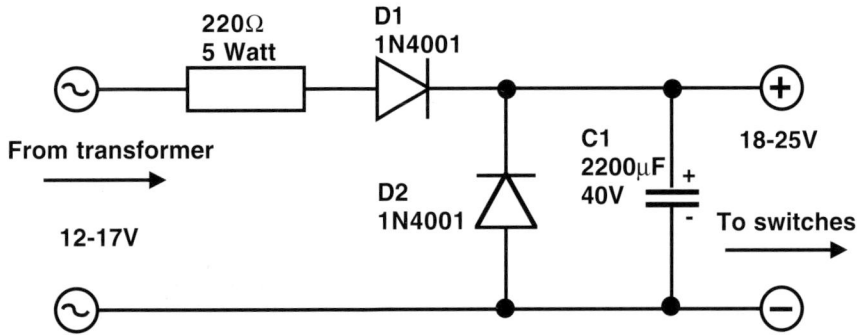

thrown at the same time, even more current is required. If one could store current in advance even a small transformer would be enough to power a matrix system. This is exactly what this amplifier does – it stores current.

HOW IT WORKS

The heart of this module is a 2200 µFarad electrolytic capacitor. It is charged by the transformer between switch realignments. Charging time will vary between tenths of a second to one or two seconds, depending upon which version you build. This stored current is used to throw the switches and it'll do it without slowing down trains or dimming layout lighting. The circuit is equipped with a current limiter to protect against overloads. D1 and D2 shield the module from switch generated voltage spikes (transients).

CONSTRUCTION

Not much of the circuit board is visable in the photo thanks to the transistor heat sink. Three diodes and a resistor are hidden beneath the heat sink. The transistor is an NPN type in a TO-3 casing. This means that one of its connections (the collector) is in the casing and must be connected electrically to the circuit board via its mounting screws. I soldered a lead directly to one of the screws, but soldering tabs can be used. They fit under the nuts and are easier to solder to, that than to the screws themselves.

CONNECTIONS

The module's plus output is connected to the switches' respective push-button controls. The minus is connected to the switches' common ground. This ground lead is often black.

Components	USA	UK
3 diodes 1N4001	276-1101	3 QL73Q
1 resistor 470Ω/0.25W	271-1317	1 M470R
1 transistor 2N3055	276-2041	1 YH98G
1 heat sink 4.8°C/W TO-3*	6015C	1 FG51F
1 capacitor 2200µF/25V	272-1020	1 FB90X
1 experimental perfboard	276-1395	1 JP47B
1 card-edge-connector	276-1564	1 FL86T
* Jameco		

Traffic lights

Functioning traffic lights have long been a wish of many model railroaders. In this chapter we'll be building a complete, functioning system. It's one of the more complex projects in the book and is not recommended as a first project for the novice.

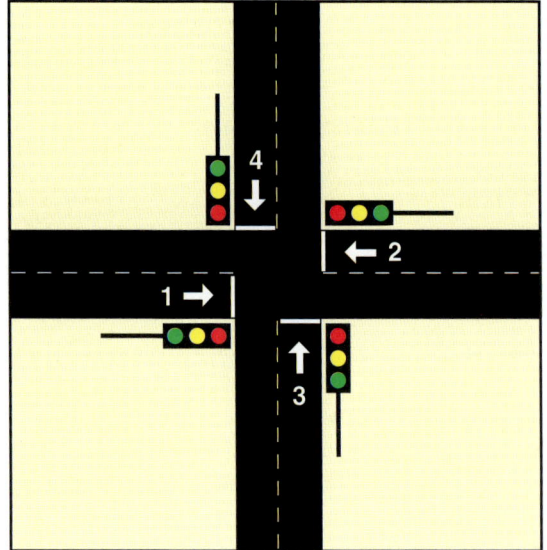

In the pre-integrated circuit days a model railroad with working traffic signals was a rarity. The control units consisted of enough relays to put a good many telephone switchboards to shame. With today's electronics we can get the job done with a control module that is smaller, offers more flexibility and is much quieter.

Our goal is to build four signal units. Each is to have a green, red and yellow light. They're to be placed in a four-way intersection. We need a signalling sequence that gives green from both directions for through traffic and at the same time, red for cross traffic. After ten seconds, the green should switch to yellow for about one second. This is to be followed by a red signal for through traffic and a green for cross traffic. The sequence should be repeated every ten seconds.

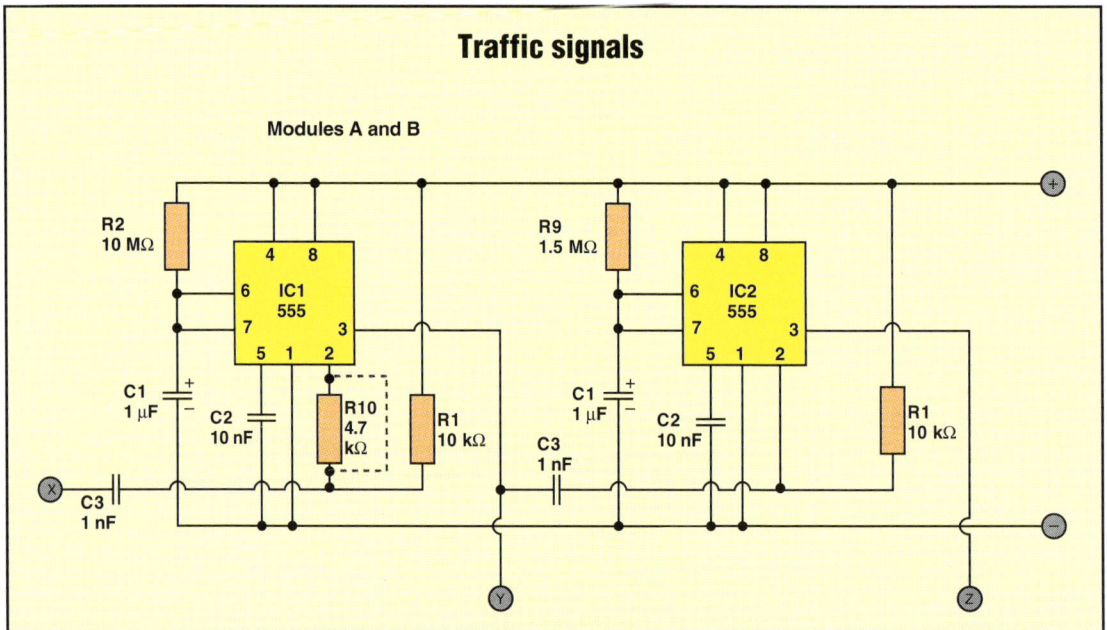

Traffic signals

Traffic signals

Module C

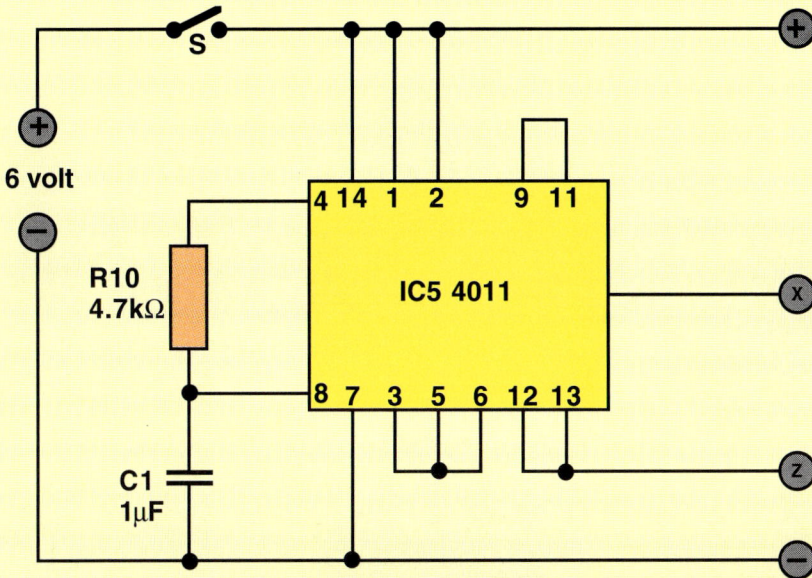

6 volt

R10
4.7kΩ

IC5 4011

4 14 1 2   9 11

8 7 3 5 6 12 13

C1
1µF

X

Z

Traffic signals

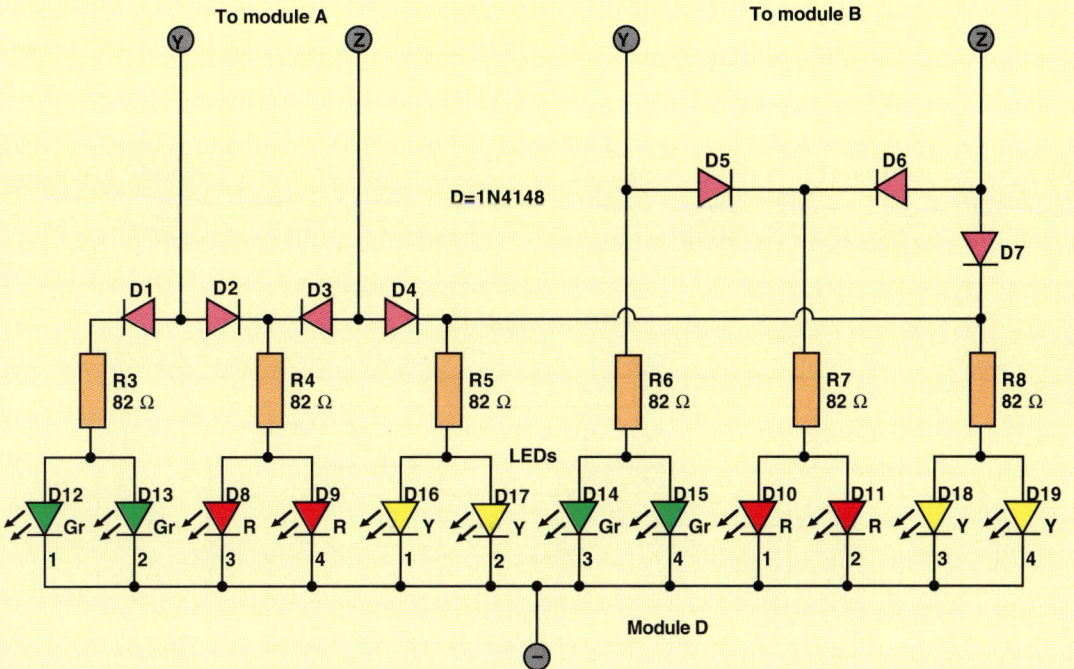

To module A

To module B

D=1N4148

D5   D6

D7

D1   D2   D3   D4

R3
82 Ω

R4
82 Ω

R5
82 Ω

R6
82 Ω

R7
82 Ω

R8
82 Ω

LEDs

D12   D13   D8   D9   D16   D17   D14   D15   D10   D11   D18   D19
Gr   Gr   R   R   Y   Y   Gr   Gr   R   R   Y   Y
1   2   3   4   1   2   3   4   1   2   3   4

Module D

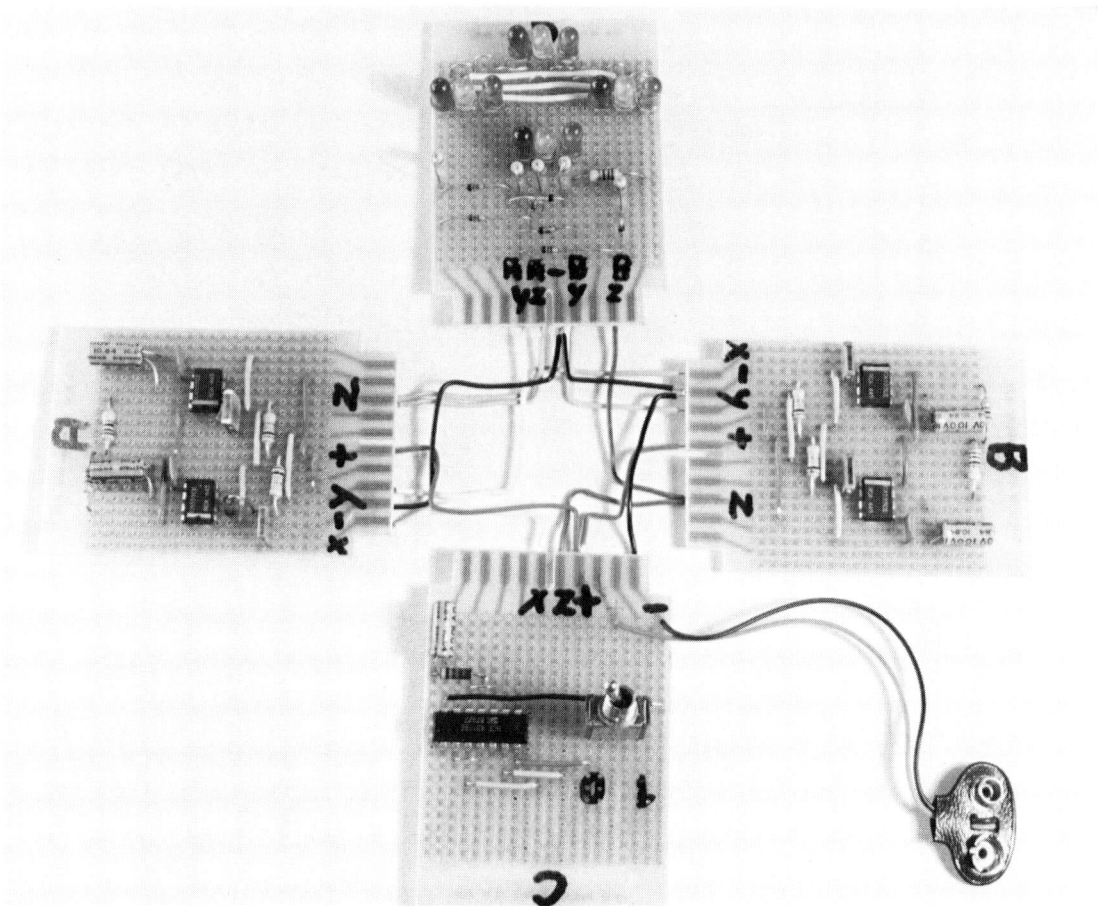

HOW IT WORKS

We have a total of four signal states to regulate. Each of them uses an electronic timer relay built around an IC 555. The IC is used as a monostable switch with its accompanying RC circuit of resistors and capacitors. The two red/green states have a time constant of about ten seconds and the red/yellow of about one second. We vary the times by using either a1.5 MΩ or a 10 MΩ resister between IC 555's pins 4 and 6. All timer modules are connected in a ring and influence one another.

Module C, built around IC5 4011, is a

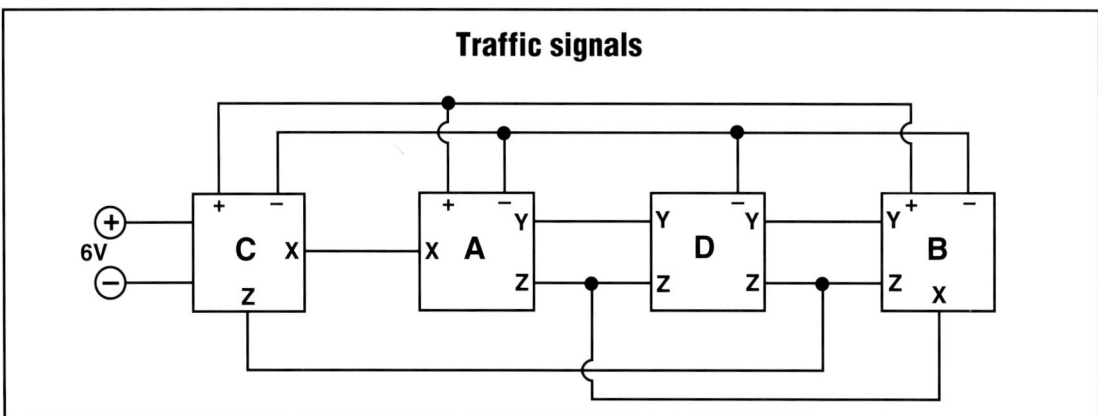

Traffic signals

starter circuit. It's only function is to start the signalling process. After this, modules A and B take over operations.

CONSTRUCTION

Modules A and B differ only in the sense that the resistors at pin 2 module a requires a 4.7 KΩ resistor here while B has no resistor. You'll need two modules of each. On my prototype, I mounted the signal LEDs on a PC board. While you'll be mounting your own on signal posts, you may wish to build a LED module for testing purposes. It would come in handy if you decide to signal several intersections. My modules were assembled on separate circuit boards. You can go this route or you can build all of the modules on one circuit board. The on/off switch is on module C.

CONNECTIONS

The photo shows the connections required for a four PC board construction. The block schematic illustrates the same.

The unit is powered by 6V DC. You can use four 1.5 V batteries, the voltage regulator from page 10 or, if you'll be constructing two units, connect them in series and power them with 12V DC.

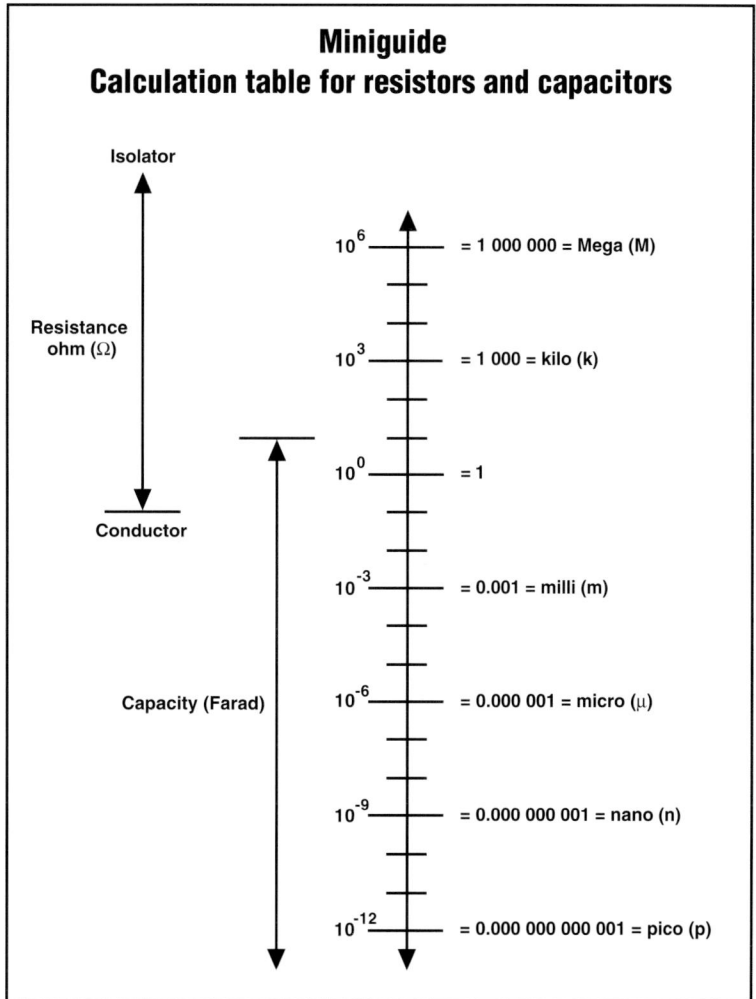

Miniguide
Calculation table for resistors and capacitors

Isolator

Resistance ohm (Ω)

Conductor

Capacity (Farad)

10^6 ———— = 1 000 000 = Mega (M)

10^3 ———— = 1 000 = kilo (k)

10^0 ———— = 1

10^{-3} ———— = 0.001 = milli (m)

10^{-6} ———— = 0.000 001 = micro (μ)

10^{-9} ———— = 0.000 000 001 = nano (n)

10^{-12} ———— = 0.000 000 000 001 = pico (p)

Components	USA	UK
4 timers IC 555	276-1723	4 QH66W
1 CMOS IC 4011	276-2411	1 QX05F
5 capacitors 1 μF/16V	272-1434	5 YY31J
4 capacitors 0.01 μF	272-131	4 WW29G
4 capacitors 0.001 μF	272-126	4 WW22Y
4 resistors 10kΩ/0.25W	271-1335	4 M10kΩ
2 resistors 10MΩ/0.25W	271-1365	2 M10MΩ
6 resistors 100 Ω/0.25W	271-1311	6 M100R
2 resistors 1.5MΩ/0.25W	271-061	2 M1.5MΩ
2 resistors 4.7kΩ/0.25W	271-1330	2 M4.7kΩ
7 diodes 1N4148	276-1122	7 QL80B
4 LEDs red 5 mm	276-044	4 UK48C
4 LEDs green 5 mm	276-022	4 UK49D
4 LEDs yellow 5 mm	276-021	4 UK50E
4 experimental perfboards	276-1395	4 JP47B
4 card-edge-connectors	276-1564	4 FL86T
1 slide switch SPST	275-406	1 FF77J

Drawbridge control unit

This is the big one. We'll be building a control unit for a working drawbridge. It'll regulate train movement, signalling and bridge movement. It's not all that difficult but you should have a few of the simpler projects under your belt before tackling this one.

A working drawbridge is one of the more exotic accessories on a model railroad. It can be used in single span applications to cross a canal or as the midsection in a multi-span crossing over larger bodies of water. Model drawbridges are available commercially. Many are motorized. They can also be built from scratch.

Imagine that a train is approaching the bridge. A small magnet is attached to the locos underframe. A track mounted reed switch is activated by the magnet. A pulse from the reed switch starts a chain of events. A signal switches to red, the train stops and the bridge opens. A real or imagined boat passes under the bridge. When all is clear (you decide the waiting time) the bridge returns to the closed position, the signal goes over to green and the train starts. The control unit returns to stand-by until the next magnet equipped train approaches the bridge.

HOW IT WORKS

The heart of the circuit consists of four IC 555s that work as monostable switches. That means that they have a status that they try to return to after activation. The length of time taken to complete the cycle is determined by the values of the resistors and capacitors connected to the ICs. IC 555s have start and stop pins (2 and 4). The operating cycle can be halted. We'll be using this feature on ICs 1 and 3 (the ones

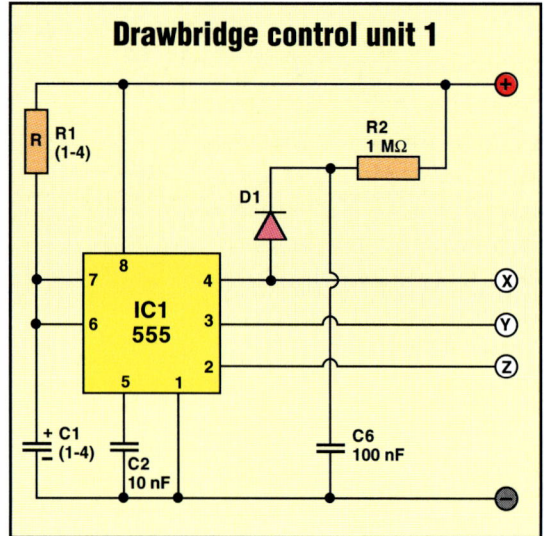

Figure 1. Timer IC 555 is used as a monostable switch. Its time constant is determined by R and C. Four IC 555s are needed, connected as shown. R and C vary as shown in figure 2. The 100 nF capacitor and 1 MΩ resistor make up the reset portion of the circuit. The IC is reset to "start" when power is turned on.

Time constants for IC-555				
IC #	1	2	3	4
R Resistor	2.2 MΩ	1 MΩ	2.2 MΩ	3.3 MΩ
C Capacitor	10 μF	10 μF	10 μF	10 μF
Time	34 s	16 s	34 s	5 s

Figure 2. Time constants vary for each IC as shown. IC1 regulates train stop time. IC2 regulates drawbridge powering time (both up and down, eight seconds in each direction). IC3 switches the drawbridge motor from upwards to downwards. It resets after eight seconds plus the five seconds that IC4 holds the bridge in the full open position. To vary these times, see the formula in the component description chapter.

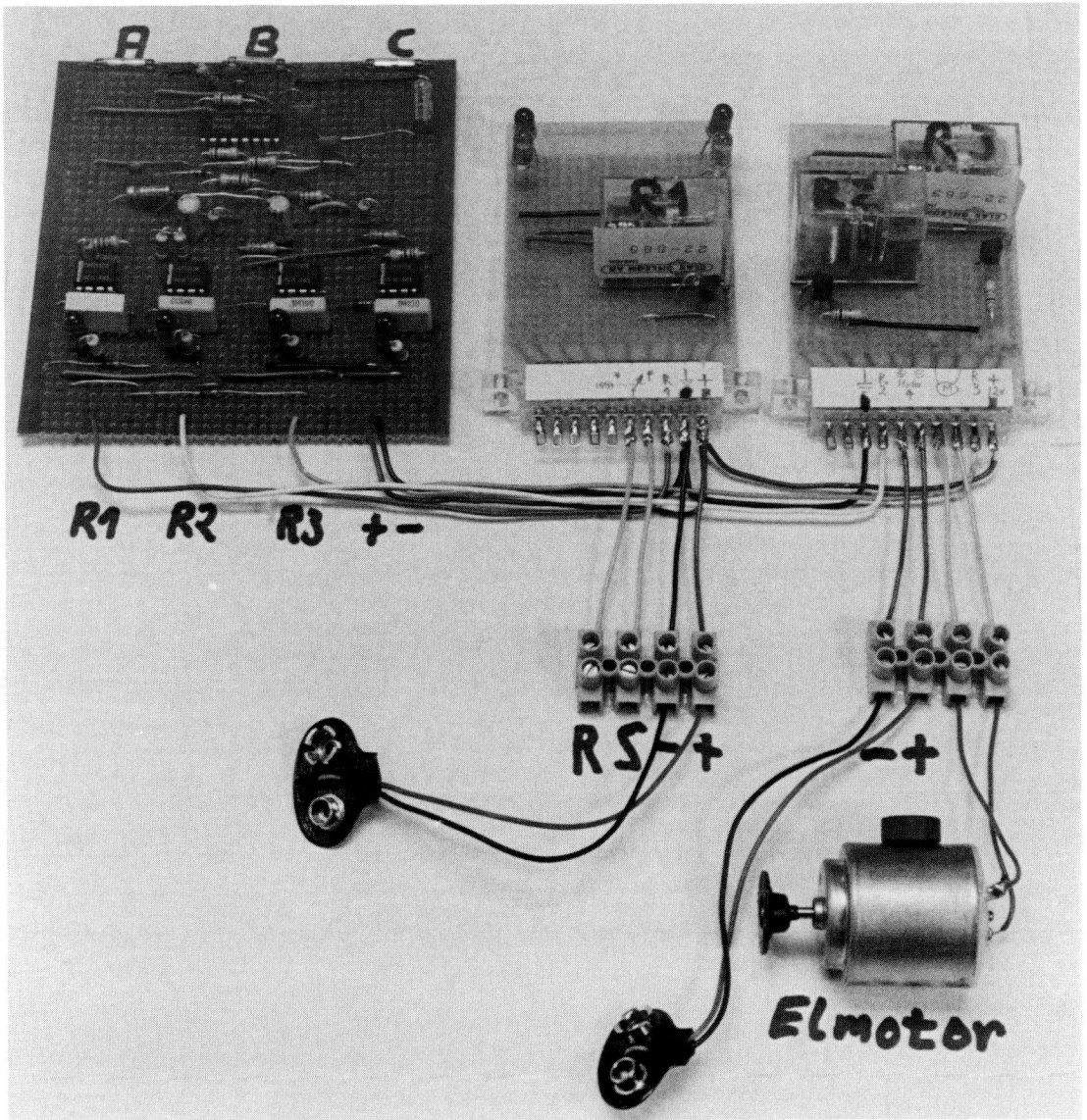

controlled by the reed switch). IC 4 regulates bridge movement and is allowed to complete its cycle at a predetermined speed. IC 4 sends start pulses to IC2 via two buffers. IC 2 regulates the bridge motor's start and stop. The diodes make sure that IC2 starts and stops in the proper sequence.

CONSTRUCTION

At the output of each IC, I have connected a LED with an accompanying current reducing resistor. As each IC is triggered (started)

and its output activated, the LED will light. While the LEDs are not necessary they are useful for checking that the proper sequence is followed and that the timing is as desired. In that this isn't a beginner's project, I haven't attempted to describe construction details or the function of each component. The photos, drawings and component list should get you through this project without difficulty. Consult the chapter on component descriptions as needed.

The various control units are divided by

Drawbridge control unit 3

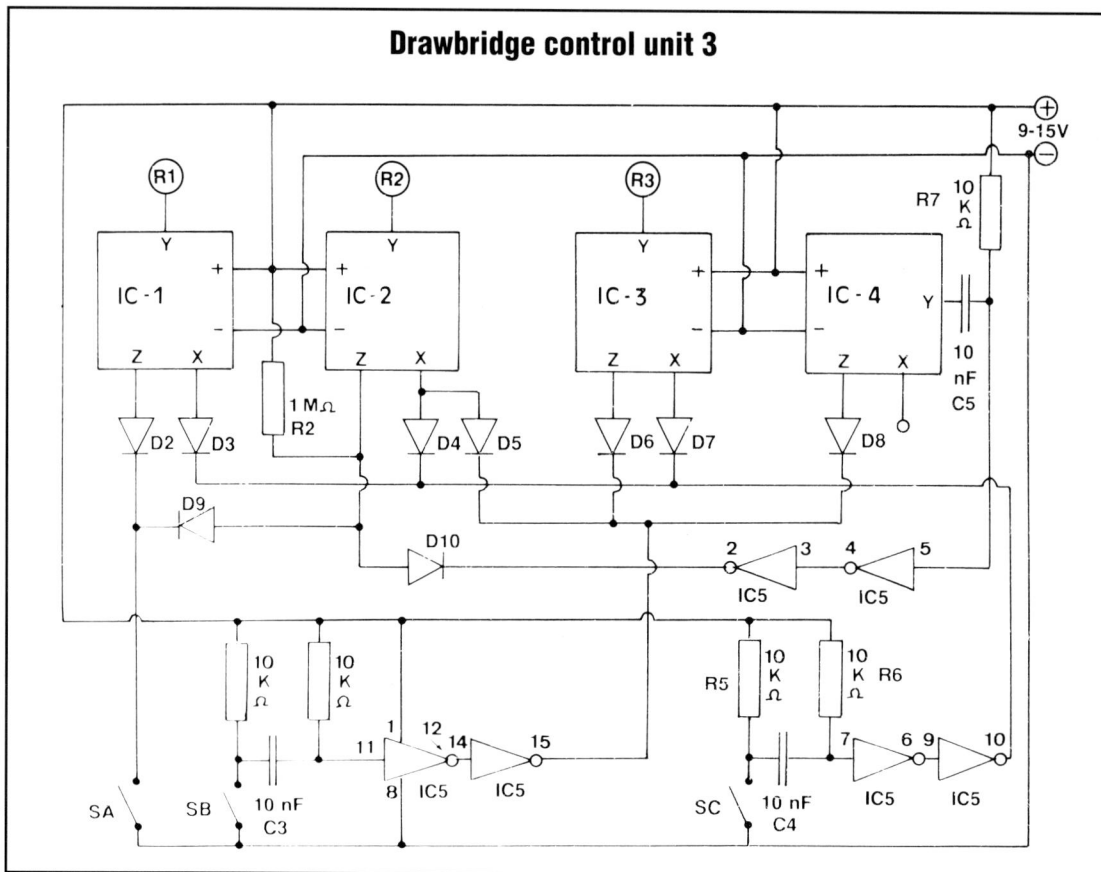

Drawbridge control unit 4

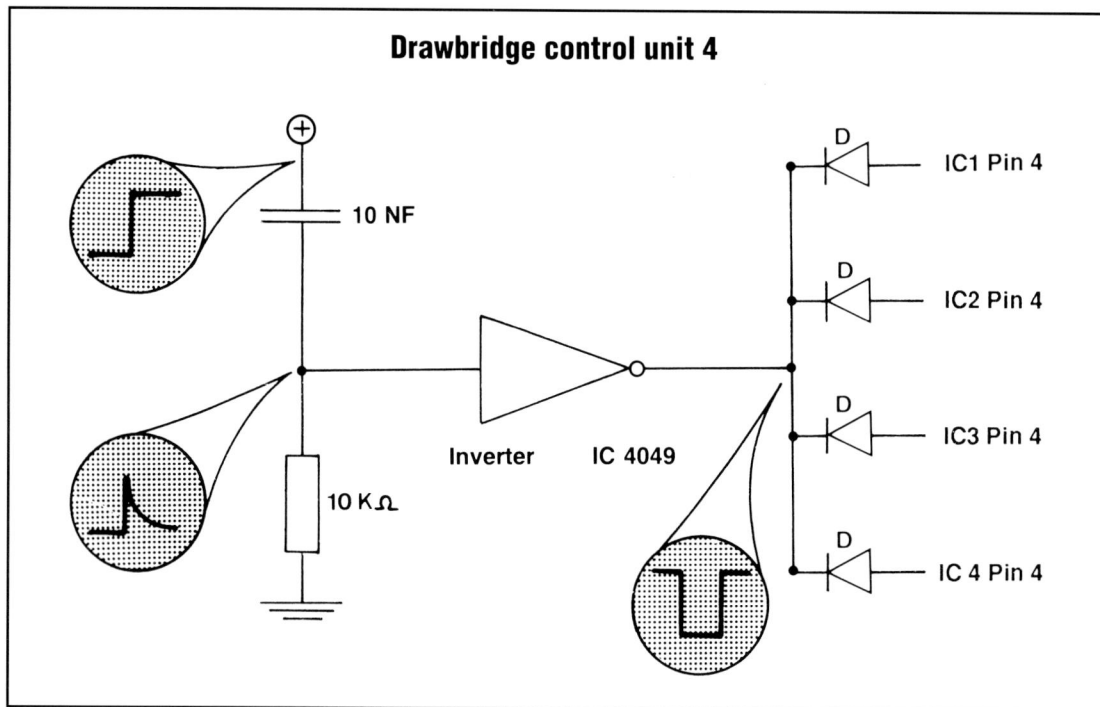

Figure 3. This schematic is of the larger of the three modules shown in the photo. The blocks marked IC1-4 correspond to the circuitry from Figure 1. The diodes determine the order in which the various ICs start and stop. Z is the start terminal. X is the stop terminal. Y is the output terminal. IC1-3 regulate relays. IC4 controls the restart of the drawbridge motor after the pause in the full open position. IC5 (CMOS 4049) contains six inverting buffers. They are used in pairs. The circuitry at B and C (reed switches) produce a short "0" pulse just as B and C close. Without this circuitry, B and C would produce a permanent "0". The bridge motor would then run continuosly.

Figure 4. It's of the utmost importance that all ICs reset to start when the control unit is turned on. As described in the caption for Figure 1, this should happen automatically. If problems arise (such as the bridge opening when the unit is turned on), add this circuit. The inverter is an IC 4049 and is the same as shown in Figure 3 (it is covered in the chapter on component descriptions). Pulse forms are shown in grey. If you use this circuit, omit the 100 nF capacitor and 1MΩ resistor shown in Figure 1.

function. The relay board in the middle controls the trains and their signals. On my prototype, the green and red LEDs for the signals were mounted on the circuit board. They'll be mounted on signal masts in actual use. The relay module has connections to the automatic train start and stop trackage (R and S). Figure 6 shows how to connect them.

The circuit board to the right controls the bridge's motor. One relay (R2) starts and stops the motor while the other (R3) regulates the direction of travel.

CONNECTIONS

See the drawings for connection information.

Figure 5. The diagram shows the various reed switches and relays and how they work in relation to bridge opening. A is the train activated reed switch that starts the whole sequence. Relay 1 is regulated by IC1 and blocks trackpower. IC2 regulates Relay 2 which controls the bridge motor. It is activated until reed switch B closes, etc.

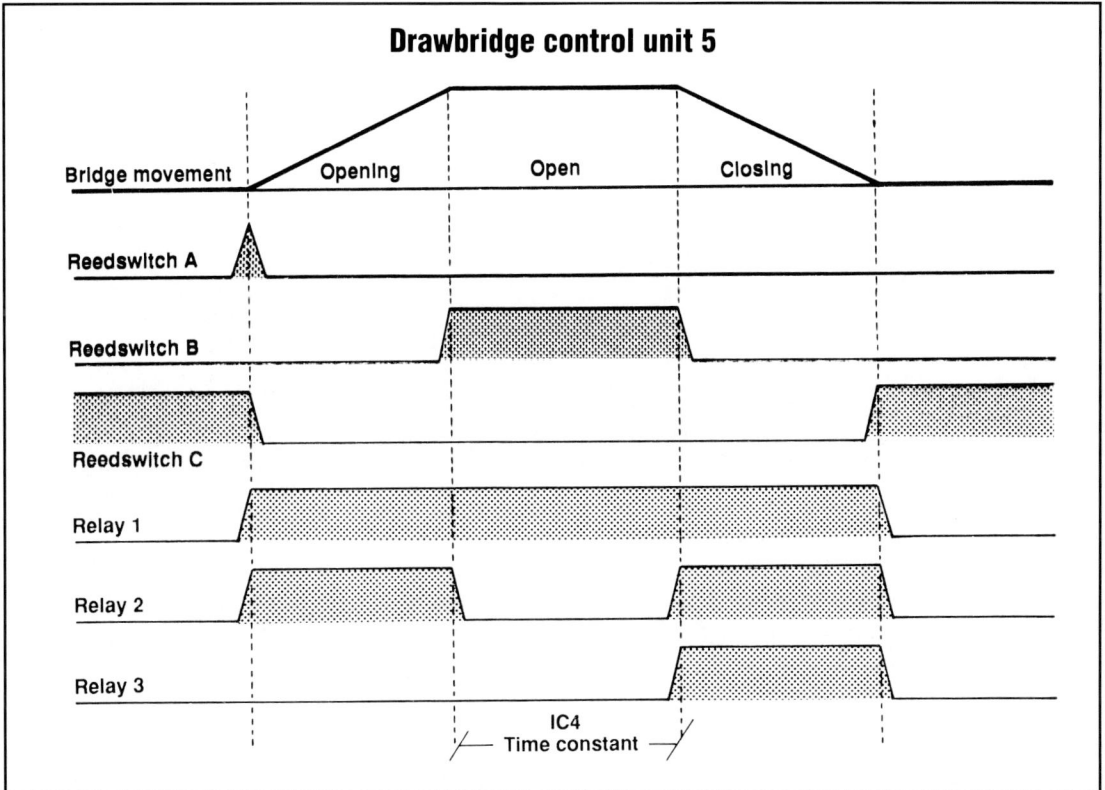

Drawbridge control unit 5

Bridge movement — Opening / Open / Closing

Reedswitch A

Reedswitch B

Reedswitch C

Relay 1

Relay 2

Relay 3

IC4
Time constant

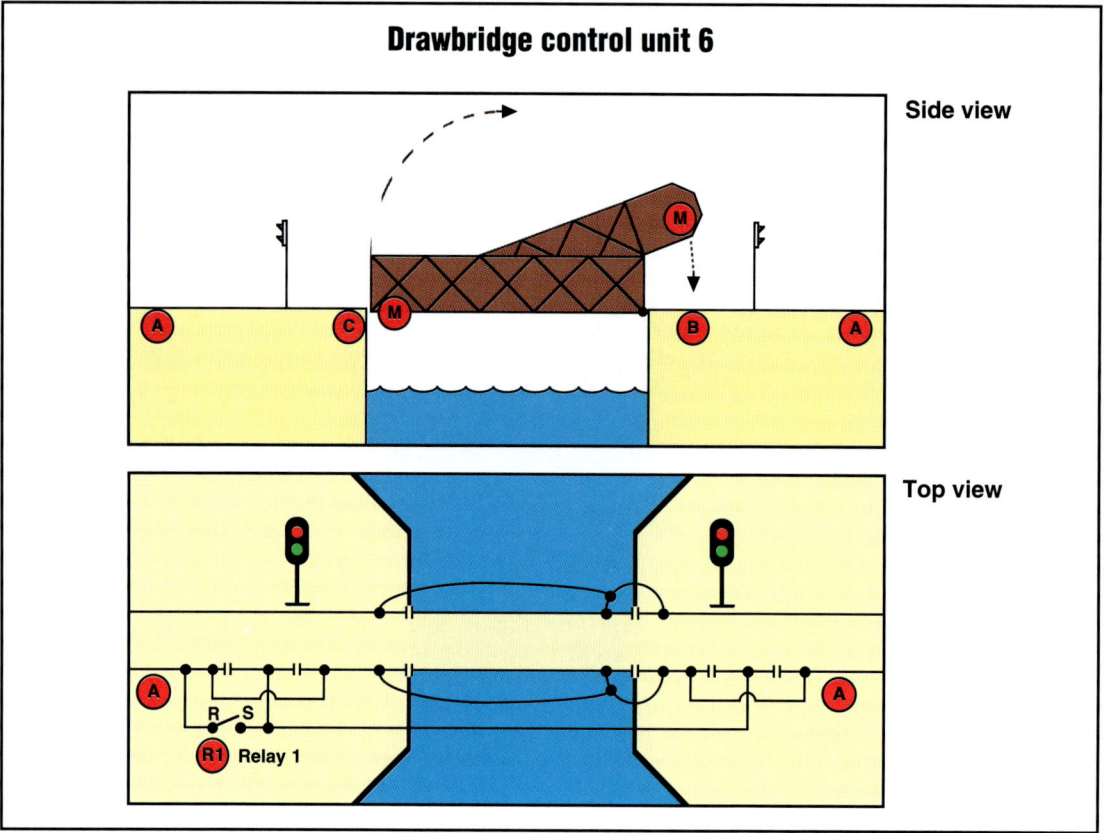

Drawbridge control unit 6

Side view

Top view

Relay 1

Figure 6.
The upper drawing shows reed switch placement. Bridge mounted magnets, working in concert with C and B, determine the drawbridges end positions. The lower drawing shows track wiring for two-way train traffic.

VARIATIONS

As usual, there are plenty of variations for those of you that desire special features.

Connect a switch parallel to reed switch A or to one of the bridge motor leads for manual operations. The motor lead switch won't halt the signalling and train stop sequence but can be advantageous if another train is to be led out on to the mainline between the signal and bridge. A switch connected in series to reed switch A will disconnect the automatic train stop feature even if a magnet equipped train approaches the bridge. Bridge status could also be shown on your control panel. .

Signalling for boat traffic is another variation that could be achieved with a little supplementary circuitry.

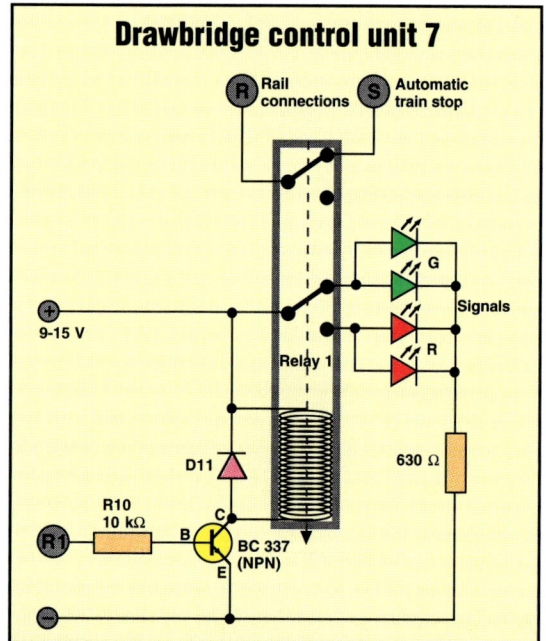

Drawbridge control unit 7

R — Rail connections
S — Automatic train stop
9-15 V
Relay 1
Signals — G, R
D11
630 Ω
R10 10 kΩ
R1
BC 337 (NPN)

Bridge control unit 8

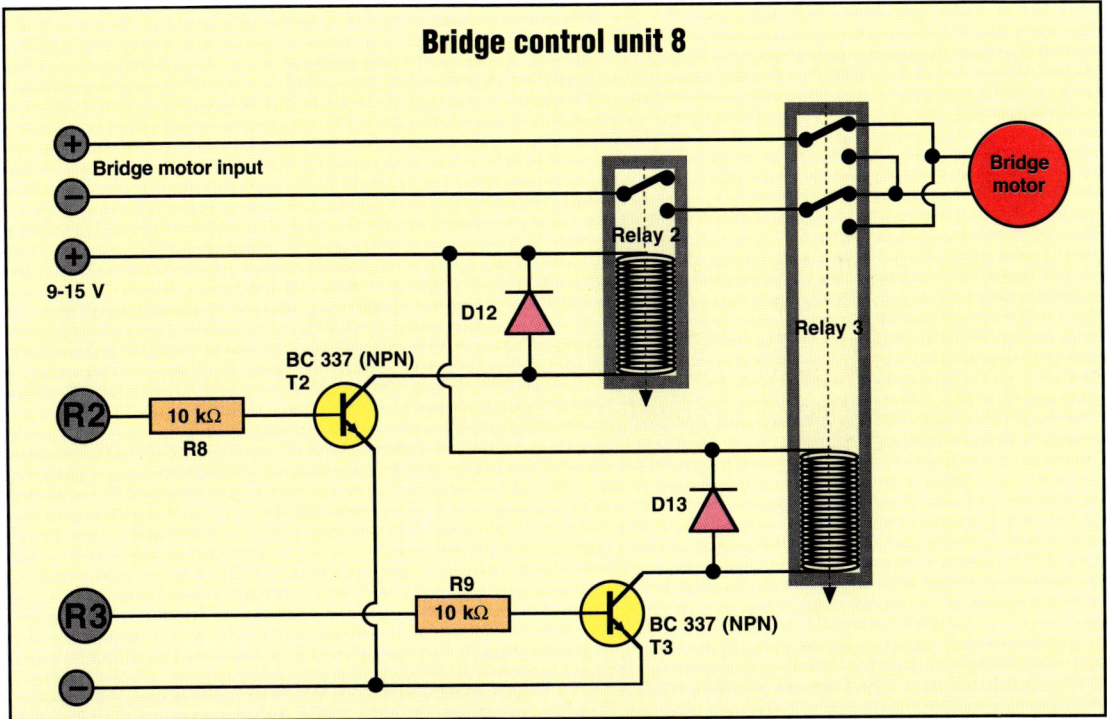

Figure 8. The drawbridge motor, control module has two relays. One is for on and off. The other regulates the motor's direction of rotation. The motor powering is shown as having its own source. This was done to permit usage of a motor of a higher or lower voltage than 12 volts. Some motors can produce interference that could confuse the ICs. An old locomotive motor would work fine and could share power with the rest of the control unit.

Figure 7.
This is the automatic train stop and signalling module. Relay 1 regulates trackpower and current to the appropriate LEDs. The diode protects the transistor from relay generated voltage spikes. Although the circuit was designed for 12 volt powering, it will work anywhere in the 9 to 15 volt range.

Components	USA	UK
4 timers IC 555	276-1723	4 QH66W
1 CMOS IC 4049	276-2449	1 QX21X
16 diodes 1N4148	276-1122	16 QL80B
3 transistors BC 547	276-2009	3 QQ14Q
7 resistors 10kΩ/0.25W	271-1335	7 M10kΩ
1 resistors 3.3MΩ/0.25W	3x271-1356	1 M3.3MΩ
2 resistors 2.2 MΩ/0.25W	1x271-1135	2 M2.2MΩ
6 resistors 1.0MΩ/0.25W	1x271-1356	6 M1.0MΩ
3 reed switches	49-497	3 FX69A
3 magnets	49-498	3 FX71N
4 capacitors 10 µF/25V	272-1013	4 FB22Y
1 capacitors 1 µF/25V	272-1434	1 YY31J
8 capacitors 0.01 µF	272-131	4 YR75S
2 relays DPDT 12V	275-249	2 YX95D
1 relay SPDT 12V	275-248	1 YX94C
4 experimental perfboards	276-1395	4 JP47B
4 card-edge-connectors	276-1564	4 FL86T
6 LEDs red 5 mm	276-044	6 UK48C
2 LEDs green 5 mm	276-022	2 UK49D
5 resistors 680Ω/0.25W	271-021	5 M680R

Drawbridge position indicator

Although this module was designed as an add-on for the drawbridge control unit, it can also be used in other applications where position indication is desired. The circuit will work just as well as a turntable position indicator.

HOW IT WORKS

IC UAA 170 is an analog/digital converter. It will convert anolog voltages of between 0 and 12 volts to digital information. In this project we'll be using this information to turn on and off a series of LEDs in a pre-

determined order. If we stack the LEDs and gradually apply voltage, the turn-on point will work its way up the stack. We'll be using a potentiometer at the output as a sender.

A standard potentiometer can be turned nearly 360 degrees. This is fine for drawbrige indication. For turntable applications, use a pot without end stops.

While we'll be using nine LEDs on our bridge indicator, the IC is capable of driving up to 16 LEDs. If that's not enough, you can cascade connect more ICs.

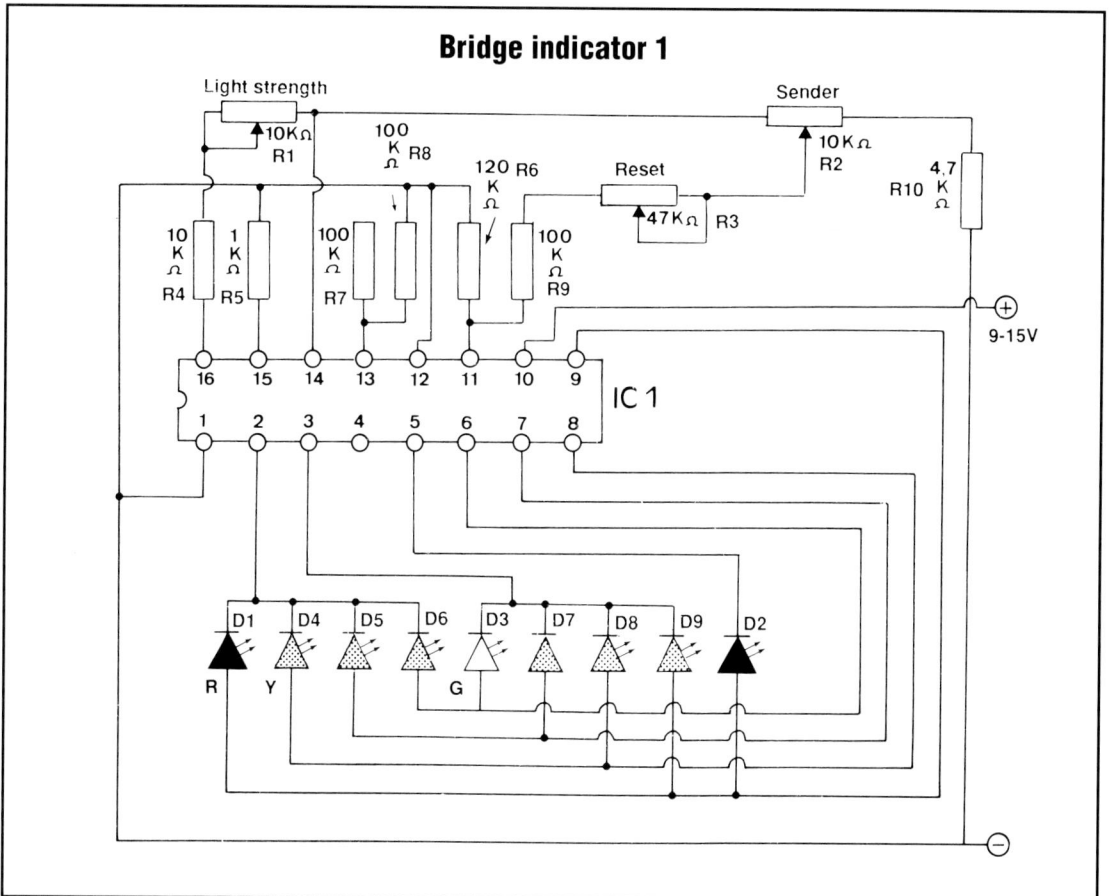

Bridge indicator 1

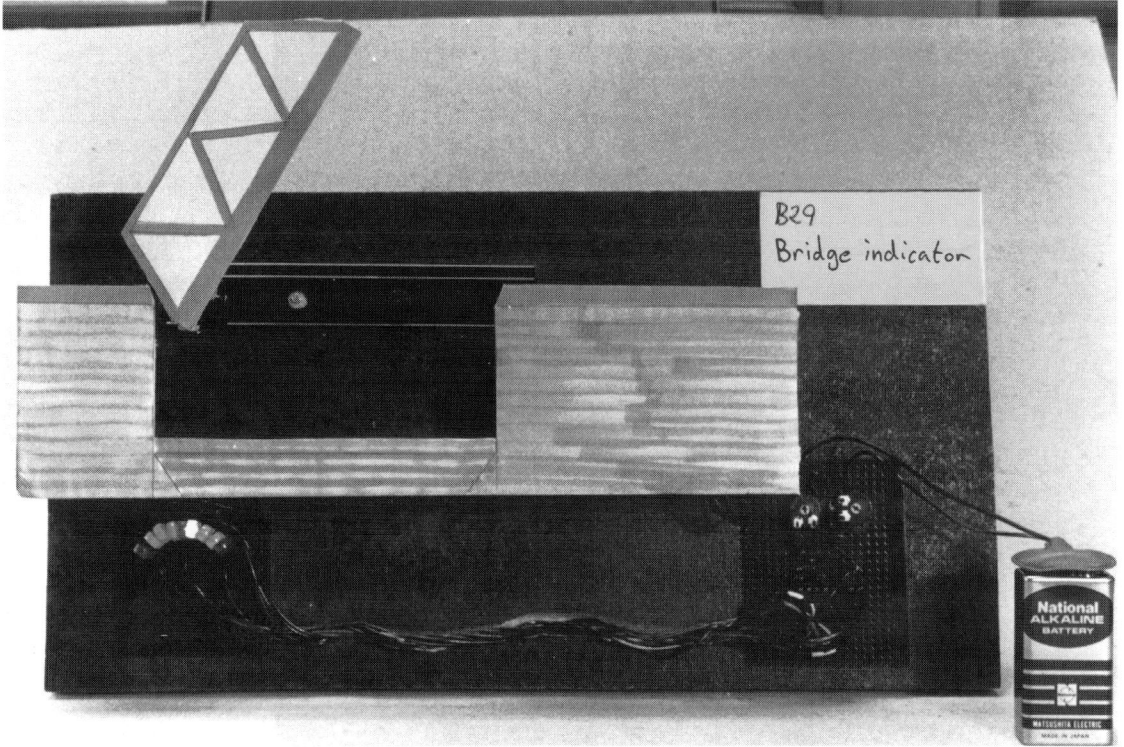

Figure 1. Connected to IC1 are a number of LEDs and voltage regulating resistors. The IC is an analogue to digital converter that turns on the LEDs in a given order regulated by input voltage.

Figure 2. This drawing shows control panel layout for the drawbridge indicator LEDs.

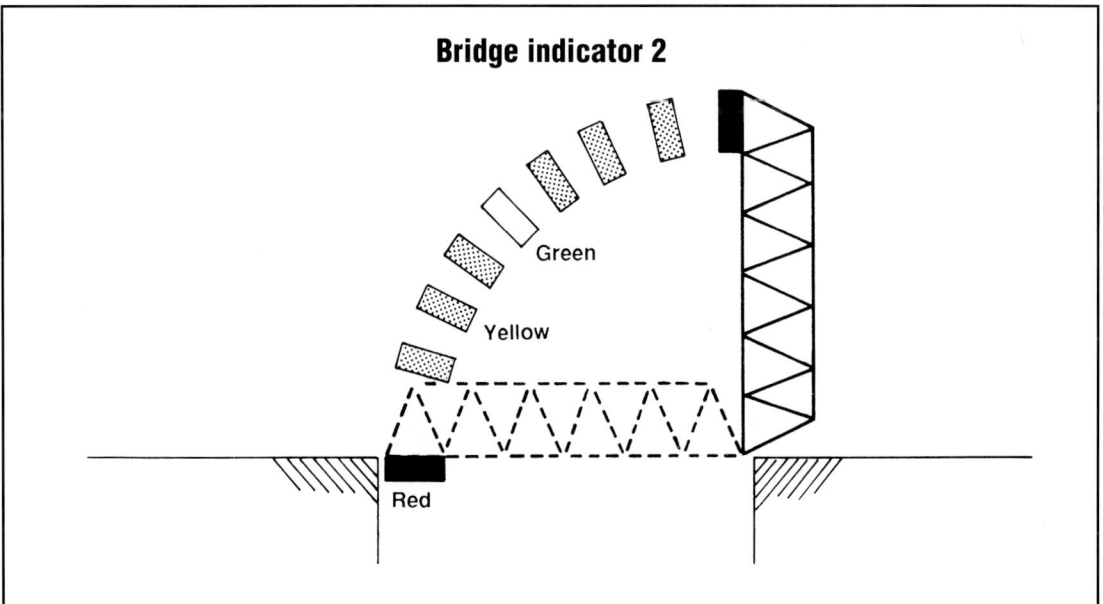

Bridge indicator 2

Green

Yellow

Red

Our bridge indicator is equipped with several useful features. Among these a reset trimpot and LED light intensity adjuster pot.

CONSTRUCTION

I've placed the LEDs on a separate circuit board to simplify control panel mounting. The LED PC is connected to the main PC via a seven conductor cable. The main PC has all of the components except for the LEDs and the sender pot.

Note that no visible current reducing resistors are used. They are built in to the IC.

CONNECTIONS

The photo shows the two modules mounted on a cardboard, mock-up bridge. The sender pot serves as the hinge. A steel axled pot could be used on a model drawbridge.

The circuit is powered by any voltage between 9 and 15 volts and, if desired, can share the control unit's power source.

You may wish to test the circuit with battery power. It's a good way of familiarizing yourself with the various adjustment possibilities.

As designed, full indication is shown when the sender pot is turned 90 degrees (which corresponds to the opening of a drawbridge). If you turn the pot more than 90 degrees, the indication will "hop". Turning the pot too far will not damage the components.

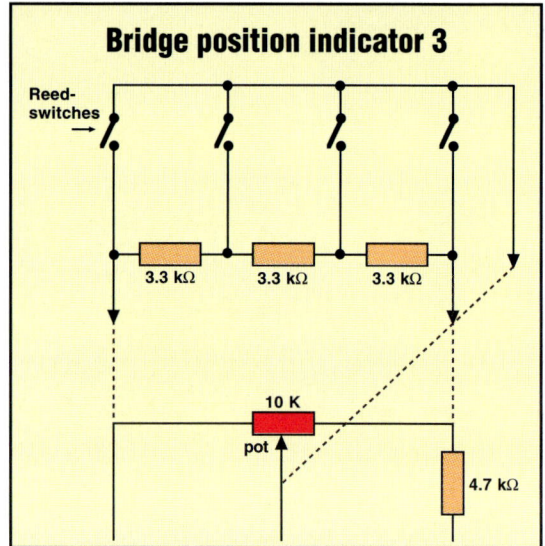

Bridge position indicator 3

Figure 3 You may find it impractical to use a potentiometer as a bridge position sender. An alternative is to use a system of resistors and reed switches as shown. If nine reed switches are used (to match the nine diodes), use 1KΩ resistors. An activating magnet could be attached to a under-the-layout lever and the reed switches mounted in close proximity, in a semi-circle.

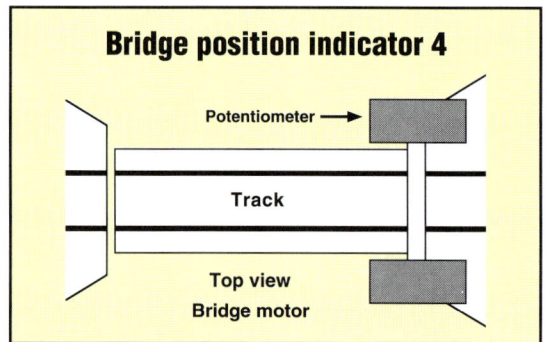

Bridge position indicator 4

Figure 4. This is a vertical view of the bridge showing the potentiometer and motor. The pot's axle is used as a hinge. It must be mounted exactly at the bridge's center of rotation. An alternative construction to this might consist of a system of levers or belts connected to the pot and /or motor, mounted under the layout.

Components	USA	UK
2 LEDs red 5 mm	276-044	2 UK48C
1 LEDs green 5 mm	276-022	1 UK49D
6 LEDs yellow 5 mm	276-021	6 UK50E
1 IC UAA 170	*	1 **
1 resistor 1kΩ/0.25W	271-1321	1 M1KΩ
1 resistor 4.7 kΩ/0.25W	271-1330	1 M4.7kΩ
1 resistor 10kΩ/0.25W	271-1335	1 M10kΩ
3 resistors 100kΩ/0.25W	271-1347	3 M100kΩ
1 resistor 120kΩ/0.25W	2x271-1350	1 M100kΩ
1 preset resistor 10 kΩ	271-282	1 UHØ3D
1 preset resistor 47 kΩ	271-283	1 UHØ5F
1 rotating potentiometer 10 kΩ	271-1721	1 JM71N
2 experimental perfboards	276-1395	2 JP47B
2 card-edge-connectors	276-1564	2 FL86T

* No Radio Schack number, but for similar function choose LM3914N
** No Maplin number available. Source Signetic's (Local dealer)

2-tone adjustable siren

This small sound module may be adjusted to produce a great variety of sounds, through the four small trimmer pot´s onboard the PCB. It is designed to be battery-powered, but there is also a possibility to power it from the transformer. If so the power module for the block traffic control (in this book) is just right to use. One can use any voltage between 9 and 15 V.

The diode is used for protection in case wrong polarity was attached. The timer-IC is used in astable mode, and produces an endless pulse train on its output pin (3). The 4046 IC is a PLL (phase-locked-loop) that contains several oscillators. A VCO-oscillator is driven by the timer produced pulse train and internal tone-oscillators are adjusted via trim-potentiometers R1 and R2.

The sound is created in a small loudspeaker (LS) 8 Ω and less that 1 W, or a piezo-electric buzzer.

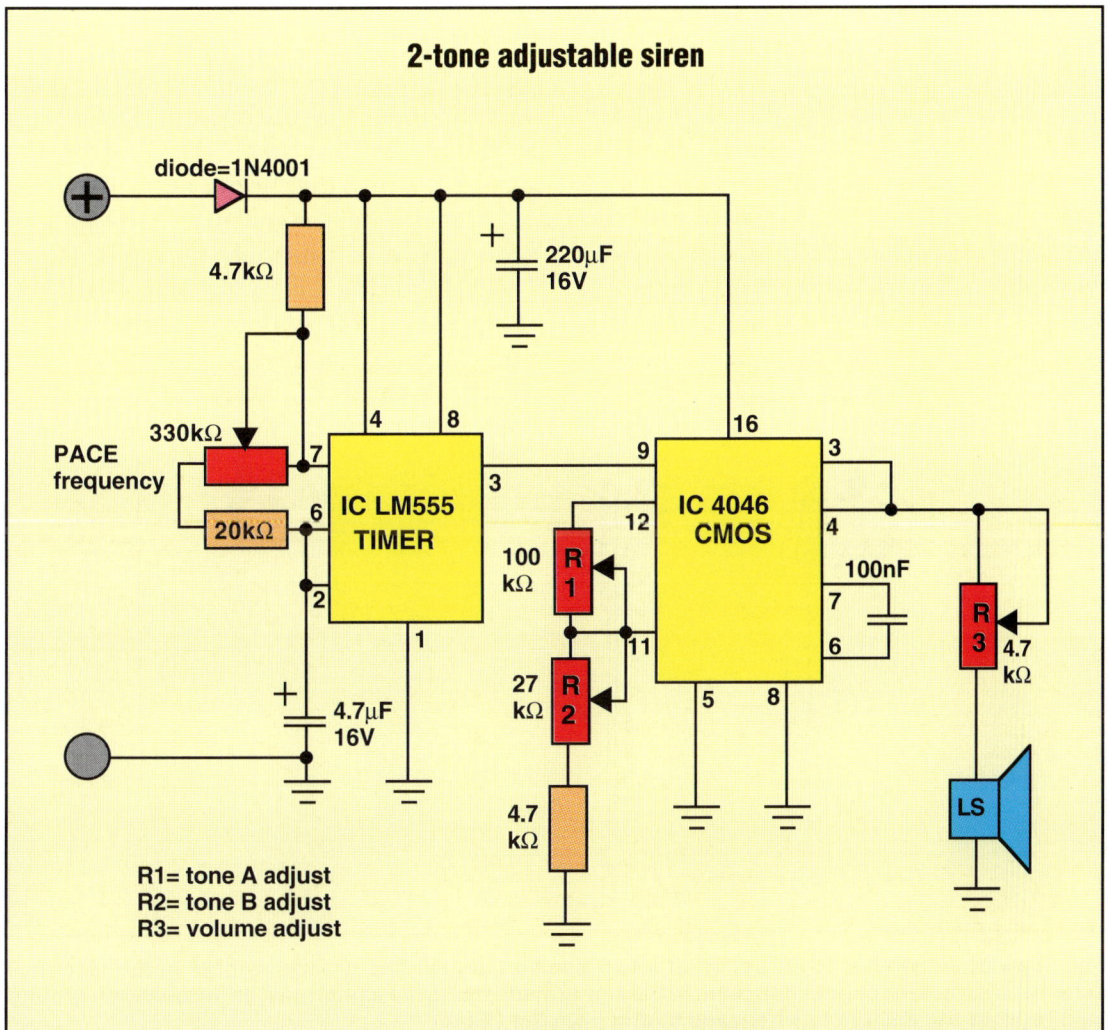

2-tone adjustable siren

diode=1N4001
4.7kΩ
220µF 16V
330kΩ
PACE frequency
20kΩ
IC LM555 TIMER
4.7µF 16V
100 kΩ R1
27 kΩ R2
4.7 kΩ
IC 4046 CMOS
100nF
R3 4.7 kΩ
LS

R1= tone A adjust
R2= tone B adjust
R3= volume adjust

Signal construction

Signalling is important on a model railroad from both the operational and visual standpoints. Although signals are available commercially, you can make them yourself for a fraction of the cost of the ready-mades and you can build them to follow any prototype.

MATERIALS

Model signals are commonly built in brass. The metal is just soft enough to work easily, is solderable and is a good conductor of electricity. Brass is available in a number of shapes and sizes.

Before you rush out to the hobby shop, take a look around the house. You may already have the materials on hand. Brass tubes from old ballpoint pens, for instance, are just right for use as signal masts. If you used a miniature headphone in one of the sound projects and tossed the wire leads into your junk box, retrieve them. The wire is just thin enough for signal wiring. As far as traffic signs go, reproductions can often be found on road maps and in road atlases.

The scale in which you model may determine if you use LEDs or miniature lamps. I usually use LEDs. They are cheaper than lamps and last much longer. They are available in red, green and yellow - just the colors we need. Figure 7 shows four common sizes arranged by scale. They can be glued in place. Use needle nose pliers when bending the legs to avoid cracking the LEDs.

CONSTRUCTION

Figure 3 illustrates signal construction. Be sure to connect the LEDs properly. Ground is marked with a small flat spot on the casing. It is also the shorter of the two legs.

Using the metal signal mast as a common ground lead will simplify wiring.

All soldering and painting should be completed before wiring the signals. A hot iron can easily melt wiring isolation. Pain-

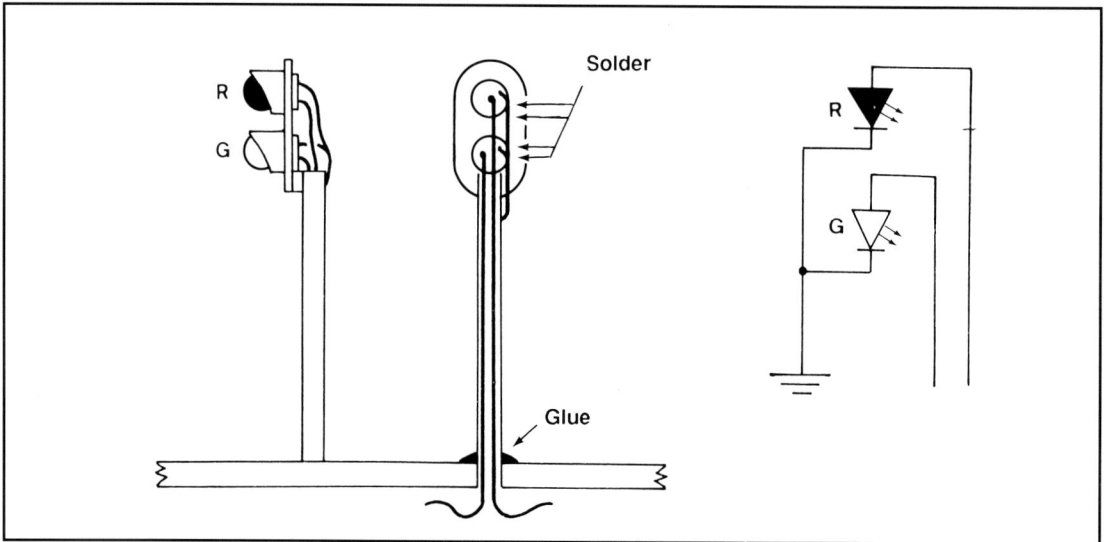

This drawing illustrates construction of a two position signal. The ground symbol in the electrical schematic shows the connection point to the signal mast. Using the signal mast as the common ground lead reduces the amount of wire leads to and from the LEDs.

ting is simplified if you don't have to paint around the LEDs or lamps.

An alternative to brass is paper. Although the finished paper signal will not be as durable as one in brass, the material is cheap and easy to work. A hole punch can be used instead of a drill for hole making. PC board is also an alternative material for some applications.

Mounting the signal on the layout is simple - just drill a hole and insert the signal. A dab of glue will help keep it in place.

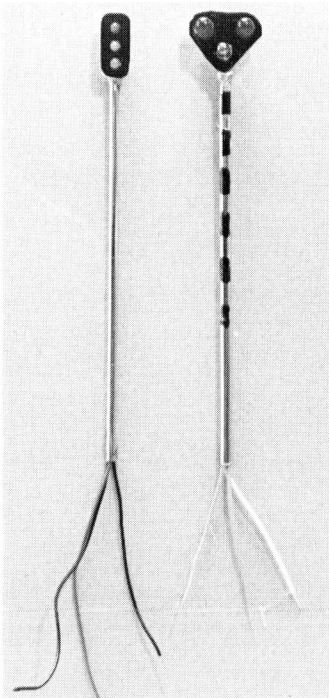

Headphone wire is an excellent source for the thin leads needed for signal wiring.

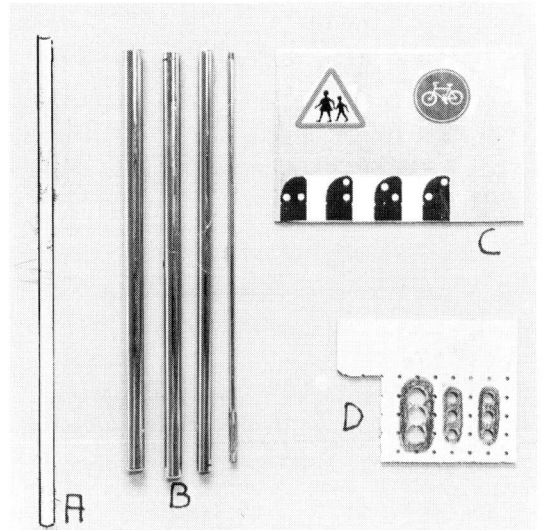

The traffic signal is in N scale. The signal to the right is built after a Swedish prototype, grade crossing signal.

Here is a sampling of signal construction material found about the house and garage. A is from a ballpoint pen. B are brass tubes taken from a broken radio antenna. C's signs and signal face plates employ a bit of thin sheet metal from an unidentifiable source. D shows a use for PC board scraps.

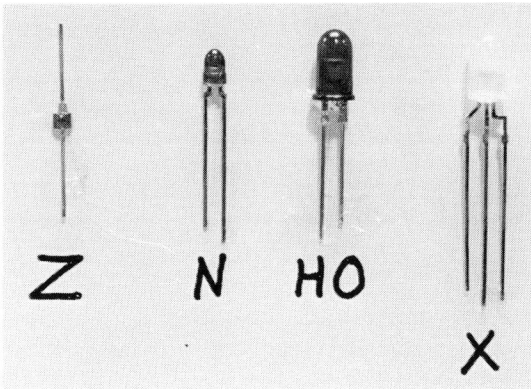

These are LEDs commonly used in model railroad signalling. The smallest of them measures just 1.9 mm in diameter and is suitable for Z scale. The LED marked "X" shows white when turned off. Depending upon how it is connected to plus and minus, it will show either red or green.

AC to DC locomotive conversion – Märklin AC

A large number of control systems and other electronic accessories on the model railroad market are unusual for Märklin modelers thanks to Märklin's use of alternating current. The same goes for many of the projects in this book. They were expressly designed for DC powered layouts. With two diodes and a little rewiring, Märklin locomotives can be converted for DC powering.

HOW IT WORKS

Household voltage is 120 volts at 60 Hertz. This means that the polarity switches 120 times per second. Via a transformer, the voltage is reduced to a safe 16 to 24 volts. The frequence remains at 60 Hertz.

The inductive resistance in a Märklin motor at 60 Hertz is nearly the same as that of a DC motor. From both an electrical and physical standpoint, it is not a problem to run a Märklin motor on DC. It's just a matter of rewiring, as shown in figure 4.

DC motors have a simpler construction than AC motors. The DC motors used on model locomotives use permanent magnets. Märklin locomotives have electromagnetic field magnets. Track current passes through these two field magnets on the way to the rotor (See figure 3). One is used for forward and the other for reverse. Rotation is switched by changing field polarity.

If the locomotive is equipped with telex coupling (remote control uncoupling) you may wish to retain this feature. If you do, don't disconnect the locomotive relay. Besides activating the telex coupling circuit, it also momentarily disconnects motor current. You'll need to connect a 24 volt power source to the track via a push-button switch for telex relay activation

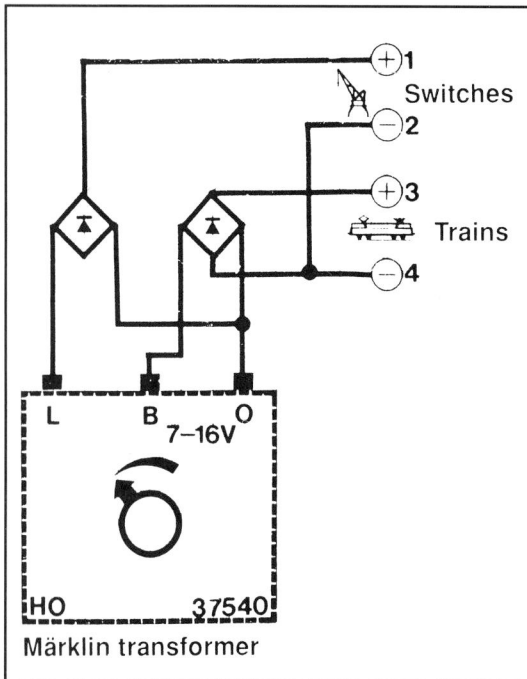

Figure 1. Märklin transformers can easily be converted for DC service by adding two full-wave bridge rectifiers to the outputs. Note that the minus terminal of the rectifier to the left is unconnected. The reverser from Chapter 7 can be connected between the rectifier to the right and the track.

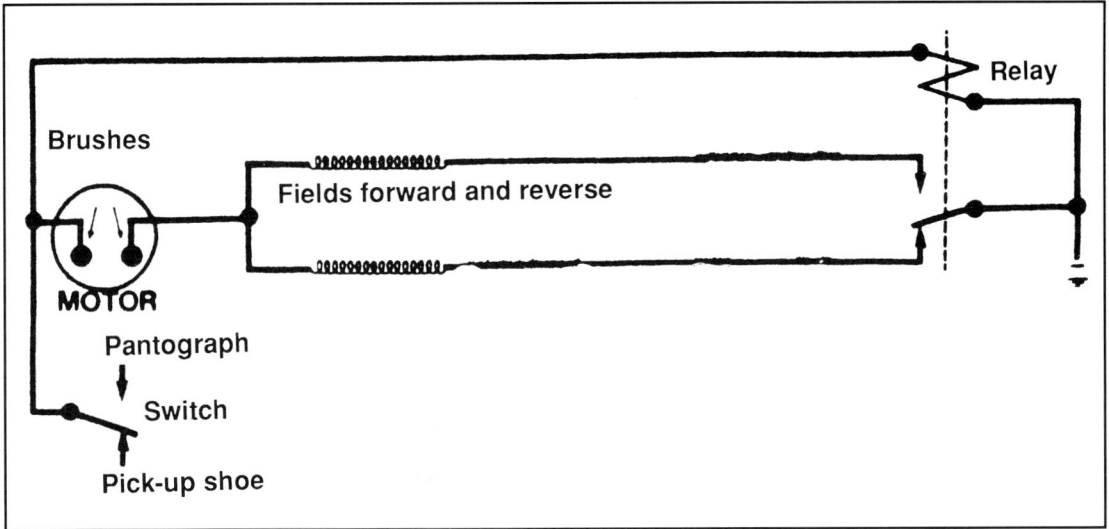

Here is a schematic of the locomotive from Figure 2. The headlights and filter capacitor are not shown.

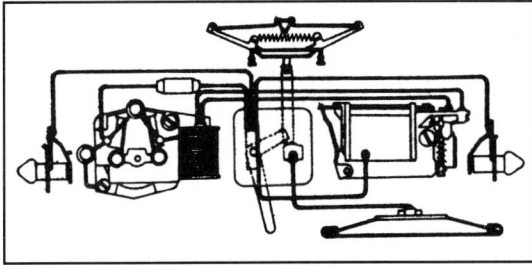

Figure 2. This is the original wiring on a typical Märklin, electric locomotive. From the left is the headlight, the motor with its accompanying field magnets, the pantograph/hot shoe switch, the locomotive relay and the rear headlight. Not shown are the common lead frame and wheels.

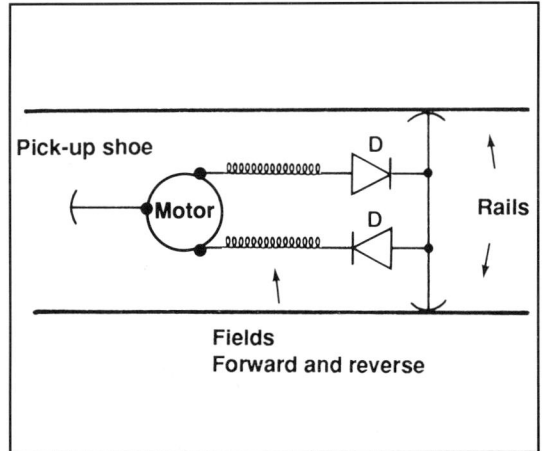

Figure 4. The two diodes are connected to the motor field leads as shown. Note that they are connected in opposite directions. In this variation, the locomotive relay is disconnected and can either be removed or remain in the locomotive. If the loco is equipped with the telex uncoupler feature and you want to retain it, see the detailed information at the end of the chapter.

AC to DC locomotive conversion – Lionel AC

This section is especially focusing on the Lionel system, but could serve as an example for other conversions using one separate field.

AC powered engines either have one field coil (Lionel) or two coils (Märklin). Equipped with one coil the power is regulated through an E-unit which is illustrated adjacent to this text. It toggles between forward and reverse mode for every hi-voltage pulse given to change direction of speed.

The Märklin design with two coils also uses a ratchet hook, initiated through a high voltage coil. The switching mechanism then toggles between the two coils in order to change the direction of the field around the armature (the rotor). Lately produced engines often have electronic modules to make this shifting since performance is smoother without any engine jumps or flashing headlights.

The Lionel design allows a simple conversion, just introducing one new component, a rectifier bridge. How that is installed can be viewed from the schematics drawn here.

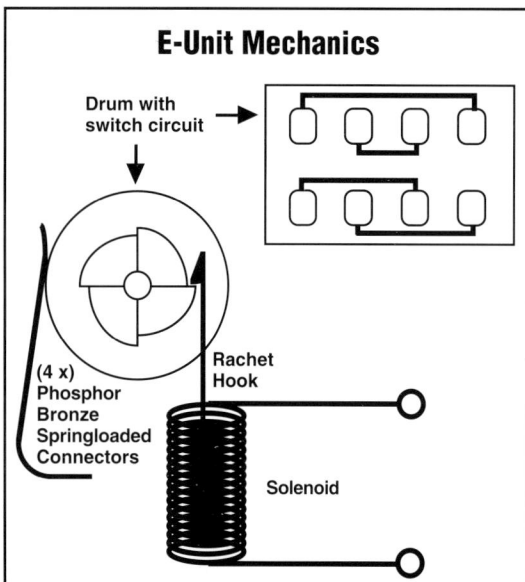

Lionel AC Motors

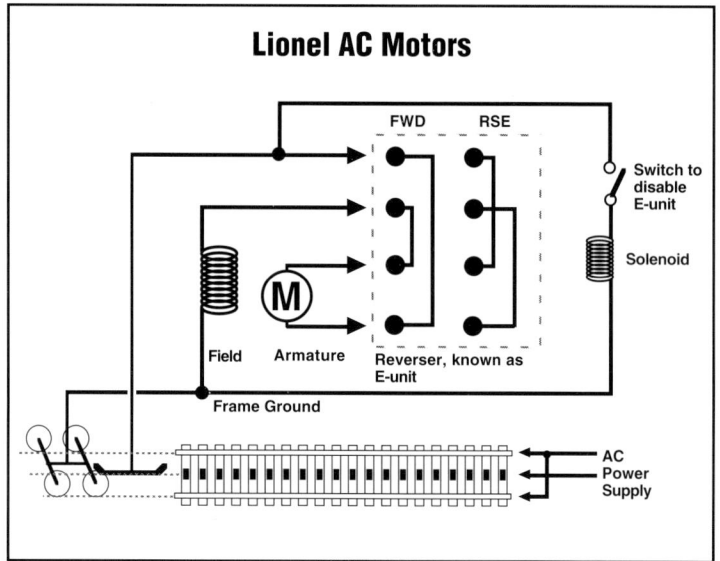

E-Unit Mechanics

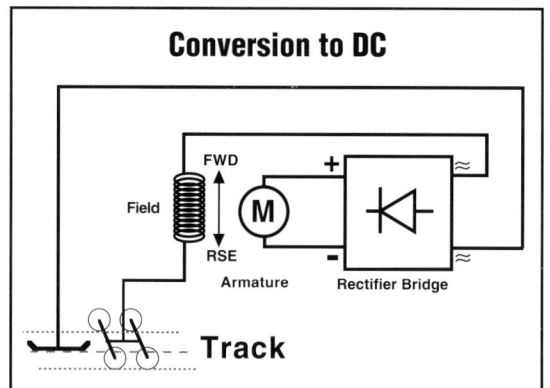

Conversion to DC

Block traffic control

There are a number of ways to control the rail blocking, such as relays, electronic modules, etc. This module is an add-on to that type of control and will provide full signal control via two leads.

A and B are the two control wires. The status guide shows how these two inputs determine the light output on the traffic signal.

B indicates if present block is occupied or free. A logic "0" gives a green or yellow telling the train to pass this section but maybe has a stop at the next. A logic "1" means stop and the red light is on. The input B is driven by the closest block module (relay ,etc).

The A indicates if then the next block is occupied or not. A "0" means no and green

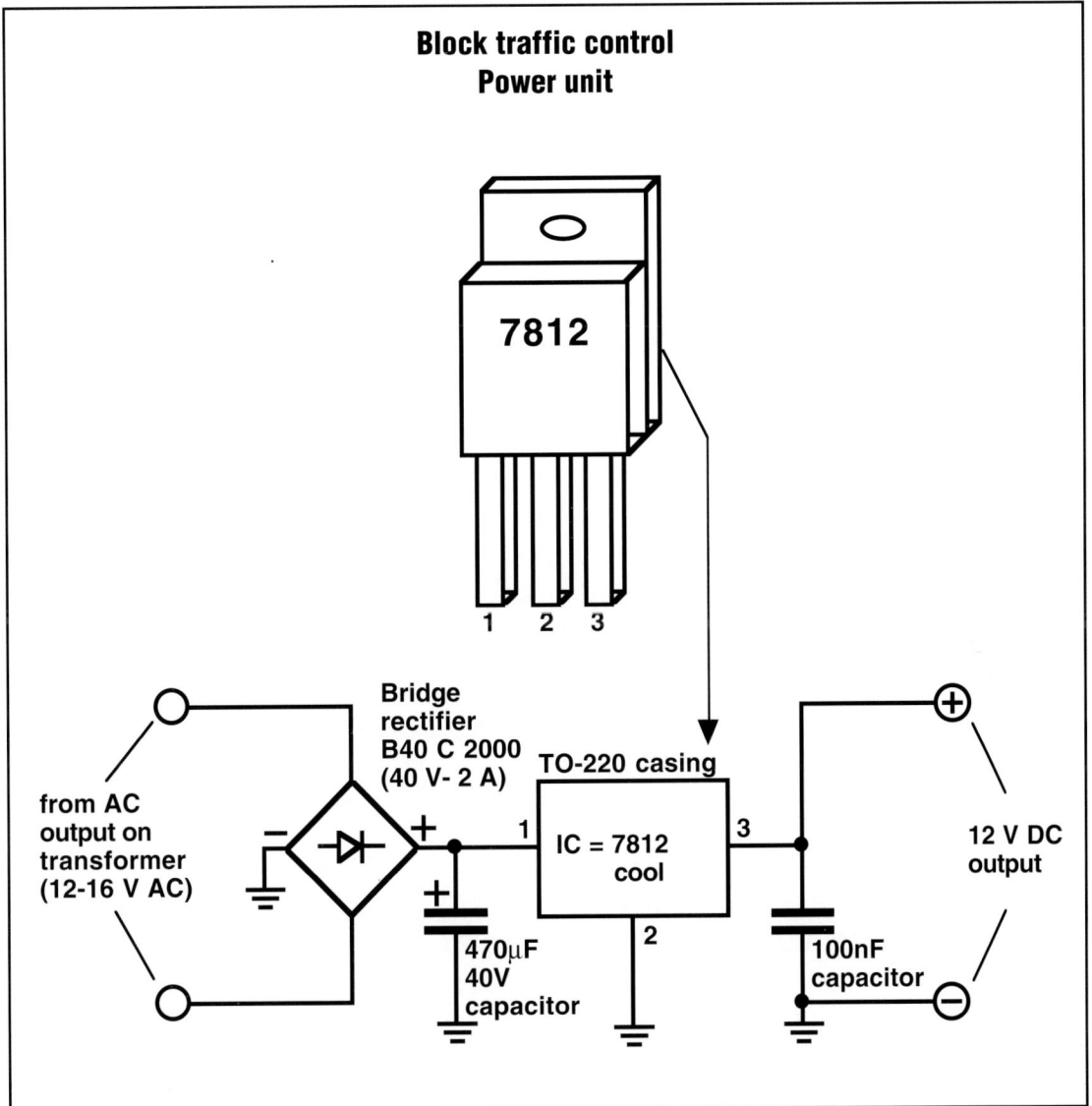

Block traffic control
Power unit

7812

TO-220 casing

from AC
output on
transformer
(12-16 V AC)

Bridge
rectifier
B40 C 2000
(40 V- 2 A)

1

IC = 7812
cool

3

2

470µF
40V
capacitor

100nF
capacitor

12 V DC
output

1   2   3

Block traffic control
Relay Module

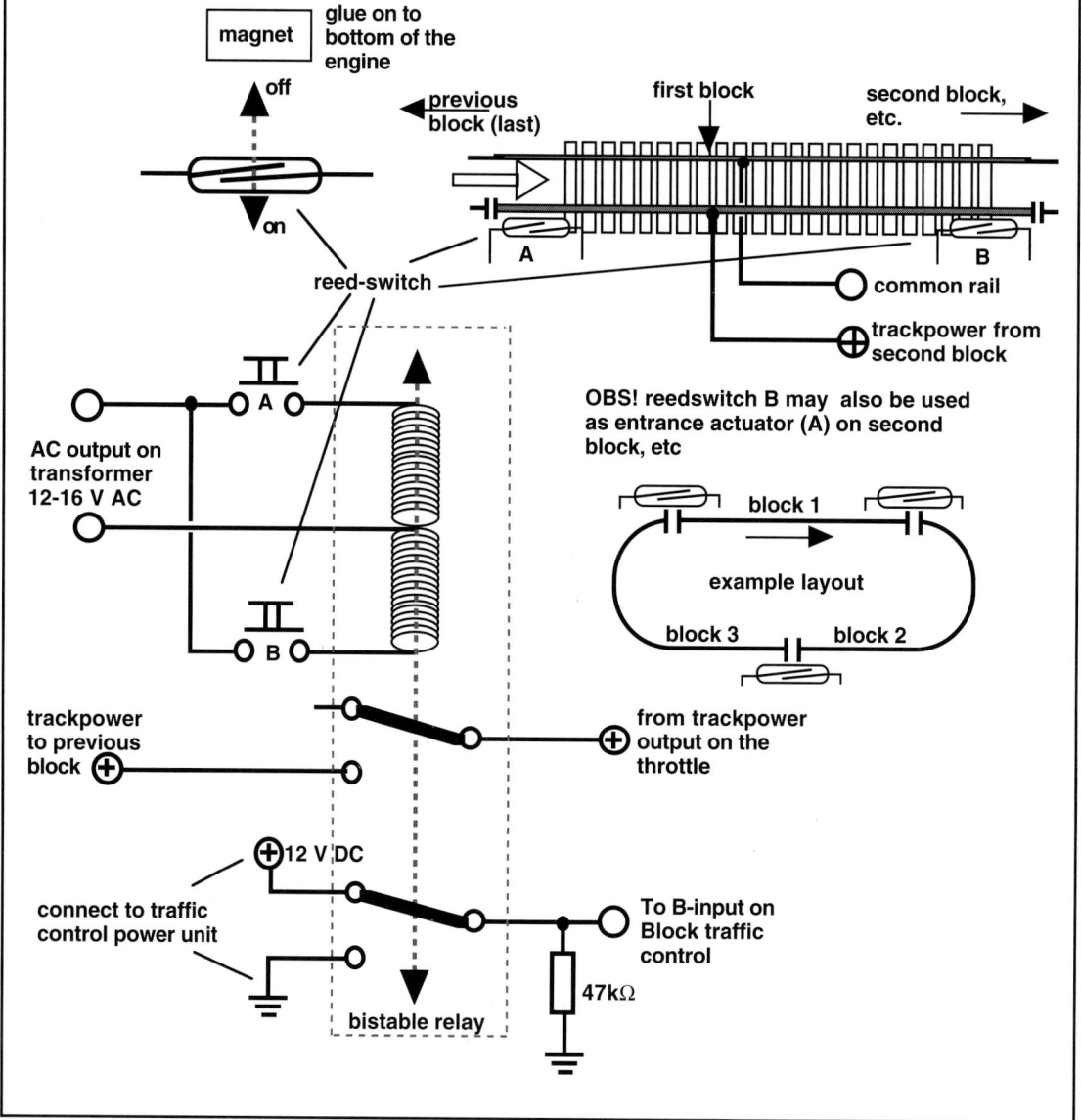

magnet — glue on to bottom of the engine

off / on

reed-switch

previous block (last)

first block

second block, etc.

A

B

common rail

trackpower from second block

AC output on transformer 12-16 V AC

A

B

OBS! reedswitch B may also be used as entrance actuator (A) on second block, etc

block 1

example layout

block 3   block 2

trackpower to previous block

from trackpower output on the throttle

12 V DC

connect to traffic control power unit

To B-input on Block traffic control

47kΩ

bistable relay

light will be on, as long as the B input stays low. If A gets logic "1" the yellow light will turn on and warn for a coming probable stop at next block. Also this assumes the B is "low".

The module may be easily tested by holding A and B inputs to either the plus voltage (="1") or to ground (="0"). A fully manual control can be obtained via cascading several signals and controlling them each via an SPDT.

It is possible to use only NOR-gates such

as IC 4001 (ref to components description section). As an alternative, the inverters of the IC 4049 may also be used (also found in the components description section).

To power this signal use the proposed power module (one unit is sufficient for 15 signals) or simply attach batteries.

Status Guide

Control inputs		Signal outputs		
A	B	Red	Yellow	Green
0	**0**	**0**	**0**	**1**
1	**0**	**0**	**1**	**0**
0	**1**	**1**	**0**	**0**
1	**1**	**1**	**0**	**0**

Block traffic control

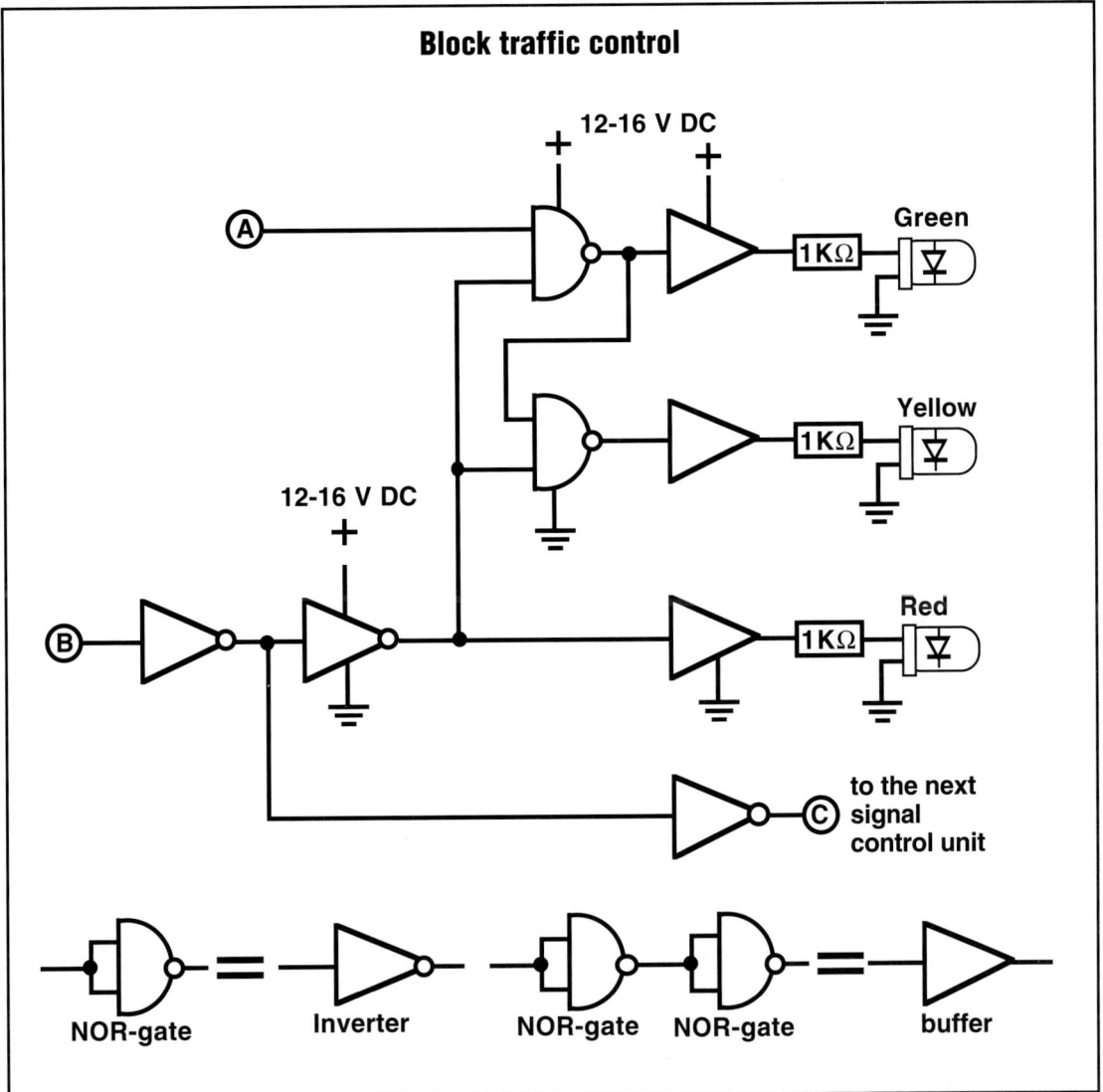

NOR-gate	Inverter	NOR-gate NOR-gate		buffer

Automatic reverse loop with direction indicator

Most likely you have already read about a simple solution to the reverse loop, earlier in this book. Here is another solution with just a few more components.

One of several advantages with this design is the indicator and the stopblock combination, if you by accident try to get the train out of the loop anti-clockwise. The two diodes – 1N5401 for H0 and above, and 1N4001 for Z and N – will only allow trains in one direction.

Depending on make and system there is a small risk that your engines only run in the wrong direction. The reason for this is then how the electric motor is connected to the rails. If so, you have to make following changes. Switch direction on both diodes, and switch the plus and minus wires from the rectifier to the loop-track.

Each railblock should have a length of at least twice the longest engine entering the loop.

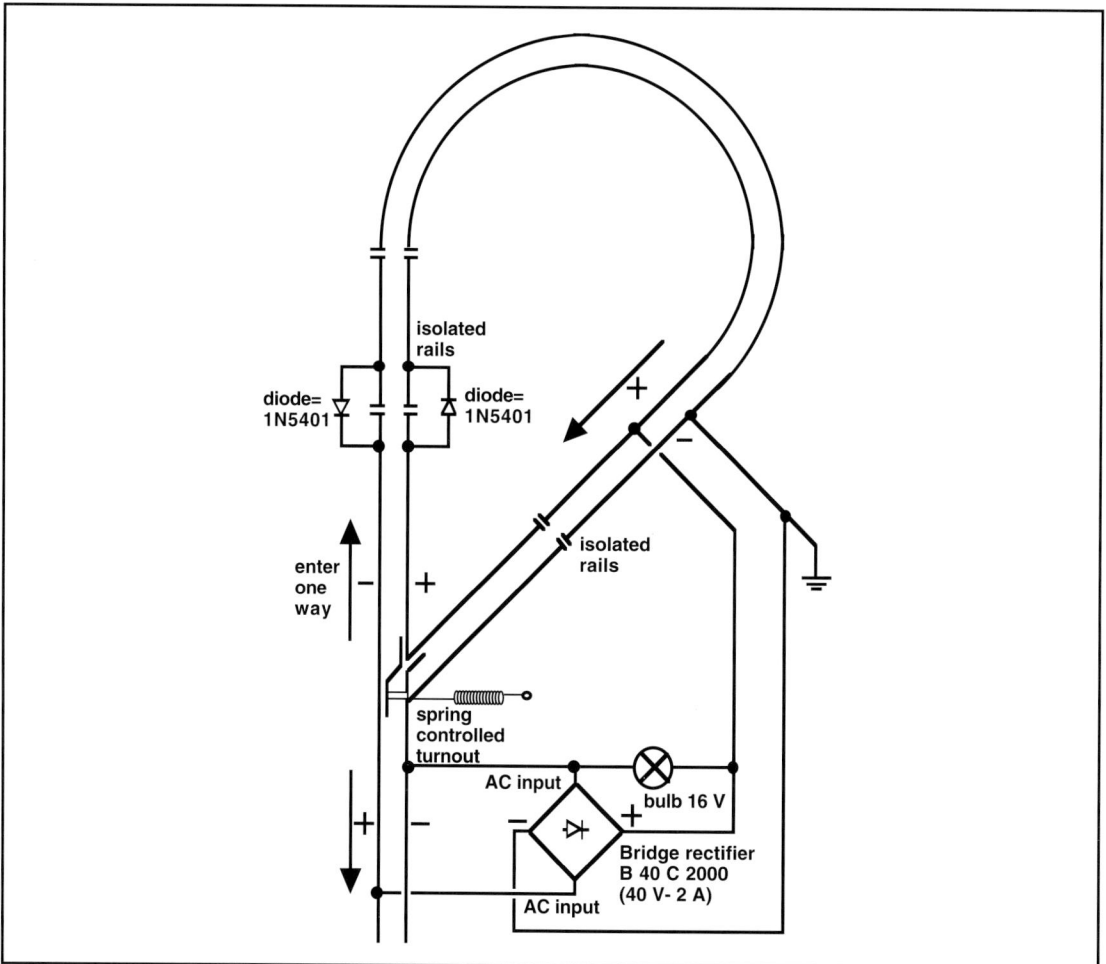

isolated rails

diode= 1N5401

diode= 1N5401

isolated rails

enter one way

spring controlled turnout

AC input

bulb 16 V

AC input

Bridge rectifier B 40 C 2000 (40 V- 2 A)

Triac relay with bistable performance

Bistable relays operating with electro-magnetic coils are expensive. Here is a cheap alternative that uses a triac (a variant of thyristor for AC). The TIC 206 can switch 4 amps of inductive load, i. e. incandescent lamps, etc. The actuators may be reed switches. These are then mounted beside the track and with a small magnet glued to the bottom of an engine. When the magnetic field reaches the ON-reed switch its contacts are short circuited and the relay turns into ON-status; vice-versa when the OFF-reed switch is activated.

The timing components have rather crucial values. The two capacitors together form a bipolar cap (1 µF totally) and the 560 Ω resistor has a maximum of 5 % tolerance. One obvious application for this module is platform lights at a station being activated during train stop.

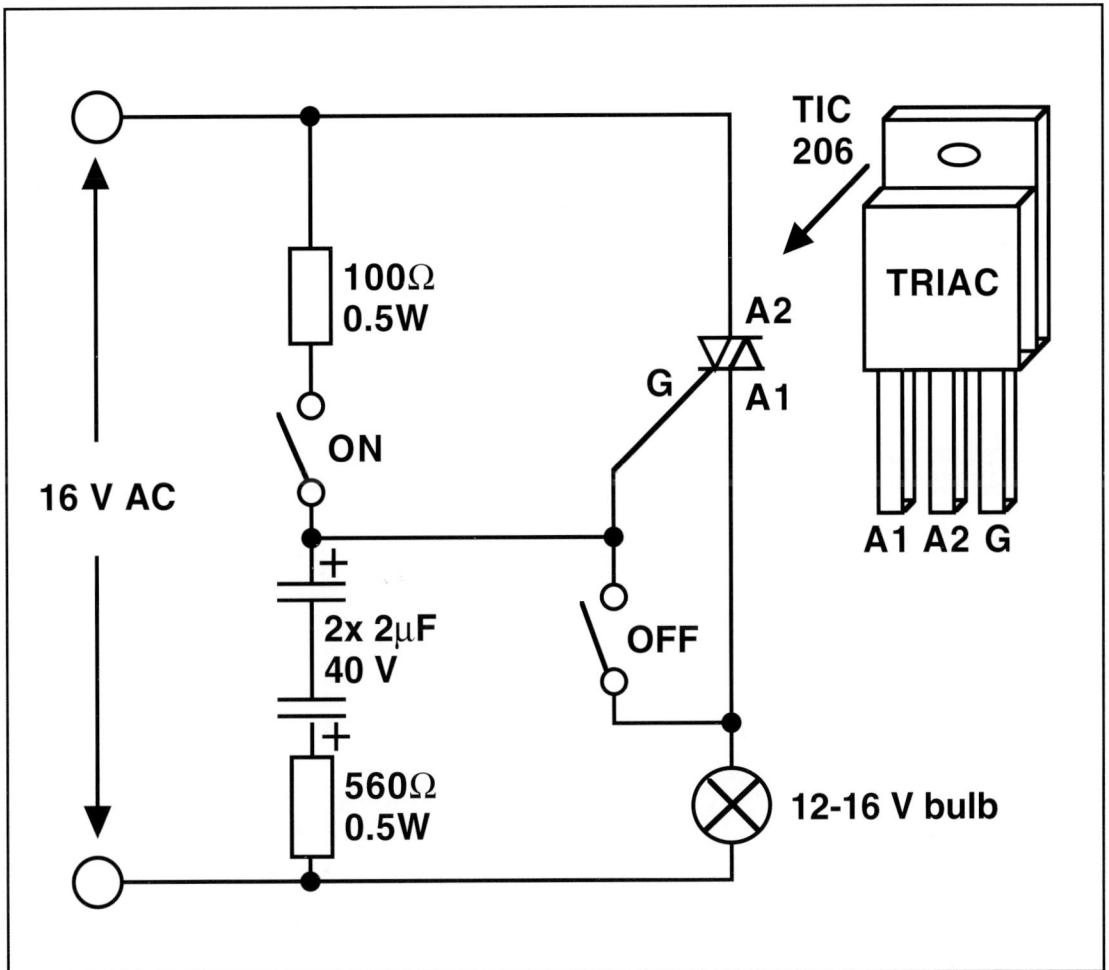

Components descriptions

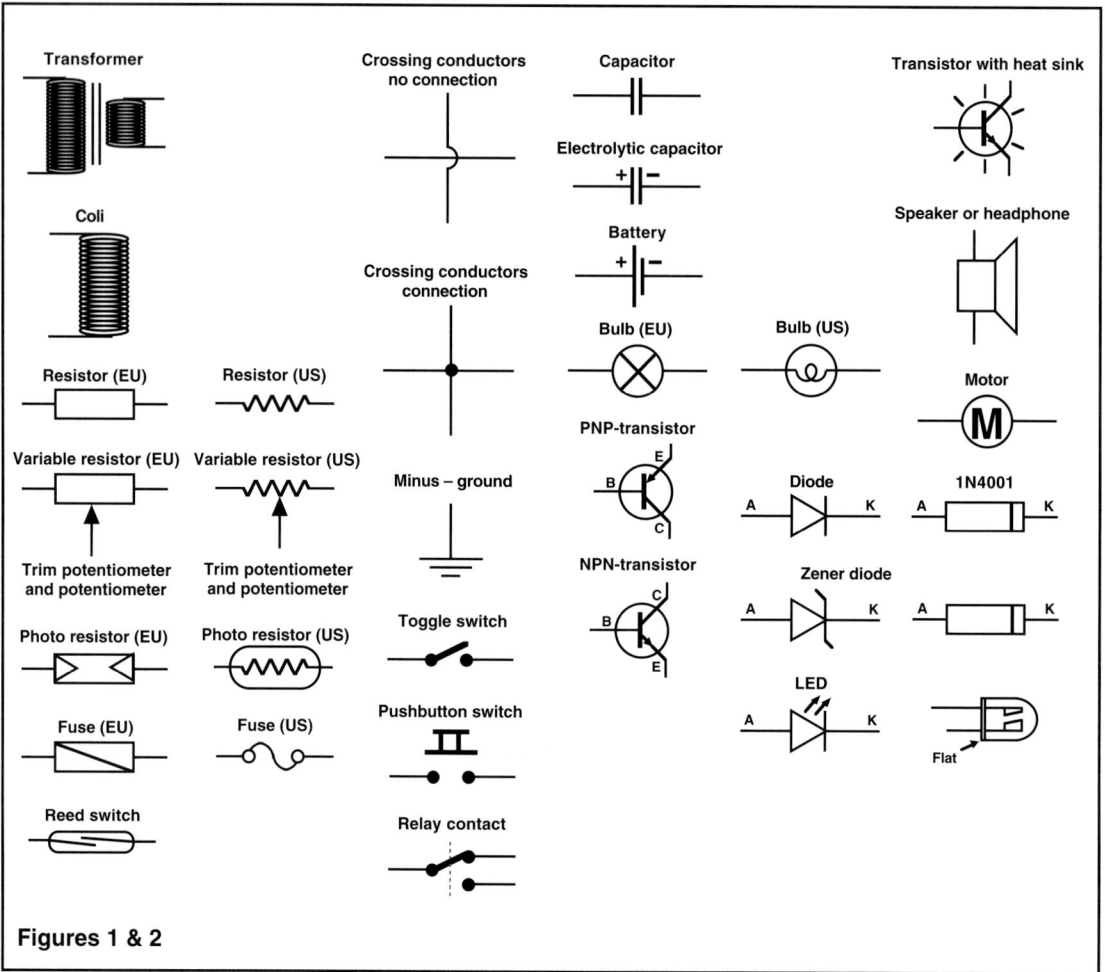

Transformer

Coil

Resistor (EU)   Resistor (US)

Variable resistor (EU)   Variable resistor (US)

Trim potentiometer and potentiometer   Trim potentiometer and potentiometer

Photo resistor (EU)   Photo resistor (US)

Fuse (EU)   Fuse (US)

Reed switch

Crossing conductors no connection

Crossing conductors connection

Minus – ground

Toggle switch

Pushbutton switch

Relay contact

Capacitor

Electrolytic capacitor

Battery

Bulb (EU)   Bulb (US)

PNP-transistor

NPN-transistor

Diode   1N4001

Zener diode

LED

Flat

Transistor with heat sink

Speaker or headphone

Motor

Figures 1 & 2

ELECTRICAL SYMBOLS (Figures 1 & 2)
Shown are the most common electrical symbols used on electrical schematic drawings.

TRANSISTOR GUIDE (Figure 3)
Transistors have three connections. Positioning of the base, collector and emitter vary with each casing type.

The transistor descriptions include information on maximum rated voltage, current and wattage. The maximum voltage is measured between the collector and emitter.

Maximum current indicates how large load (relays, motors, lamps, etc.) can safely be connected to the transistor. When running a transistor at or near its maximum current rating, a heat sink must be used. Wattage is the product of current and voltage.

IC GUIDE (Figures 4-11)
IC circuits are the black rectangular shapes with two rows of connecting pins. They contain components in a miniature format. They are often referred to as "chips". They are sensitive for overheating. To spare them

Transistor guide

NPN-transistor BC547

– Max 45V C-E
– Max 100mA Ic
– Max 0,3W Total effect

BC547   **TO-92** case

PNP-transistor BC557

– Max 45V C-E
– Max 100mA Ic
– Max 0,5W Total effect

BC557   **TO-92** case

C B E

C B E

NPN-transistor 2N3055

– Max 60V C-E
– Max 15A (with cooling)
– Max 115W Total effect

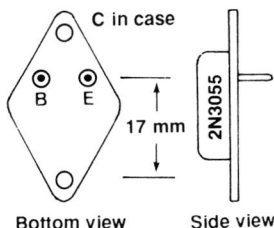

C in case

B E

17 mm

2N3055

TO-3 Case

Bottom view   Side view

Figure 3

IC guide
4001 CMOS Quad 2 input NOR-gate

+3–15V=U volt

Top view

14 13 12 11 10 9 8

at pin 1

1 2 3 4 5 6 7

Pins

Current at 10 volt = 0,8 mA

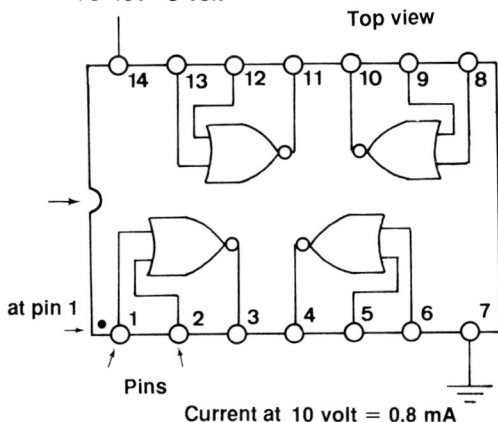

logic table for NOR gate

IN A
    B —◯— X Out

A	B	X
0	0	1
0	1	0
1	0	0
1	1	0

0 = ground
1= voltage

Figure 4

IC guide
4081 CMOS Quad 2 input AND-gate

+3–15V = U volt

Top view

14 13 12 11 10 9 8

At pin 1

1 2 3 4 5 6 7

Pins

Current at 10V=1mA

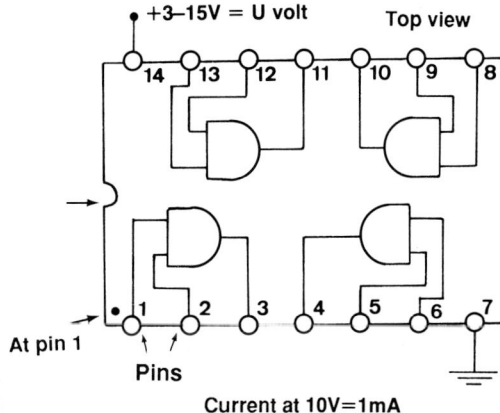

Logic table for AND-gate

IN A
    B —— X OUT

A	B	X
0	0	0
0	1	0
1	0	0
1	1	1

0 = ground
1= voltage

Figure 5

IC guide
UAA-170 wandering light
Point LED driver

Top view

U_{ph} U_1 U_{STAT} U_{ref} IN +11–18V= U volt

At pin 1

16 15 14 13 12 11 10 9 A

LED outputs

1 2 3 4 5 6 7 8
   H G F E D C B

LED matrix for UAA-170

```
        A    B    C    D       Max 13
      16/  15/  14/  13/       Min  12
E ─────────────────────
       9/  10/  11/  12/
F ─────────────────────
       8/   7/   6/   5/
G ─────────────────────
       1/   2/   3/  (4)
H ─────────────────────
```

LED 4

Figure 6

IC guide
NE-555 Timer

+4,5-16 volt

Discharge Thresehold Reference voltage

Top view

8 7 6 5

At pin 1 → 1 2 3 4

IN OUT Reset

max 600 mW

Monostabil operation

R

8
7 555 3 ─o Out
6   2 ─o START
   1   5 ─o STOP

C

$T = 1,1 \times R \times C$

Astabil operation

R_A

7 8 4
   555 3 ─o OUT
6
2 1 5

R_B

C

$T = 0,7 \times C \times (RA + 2RB)$

Figure 7

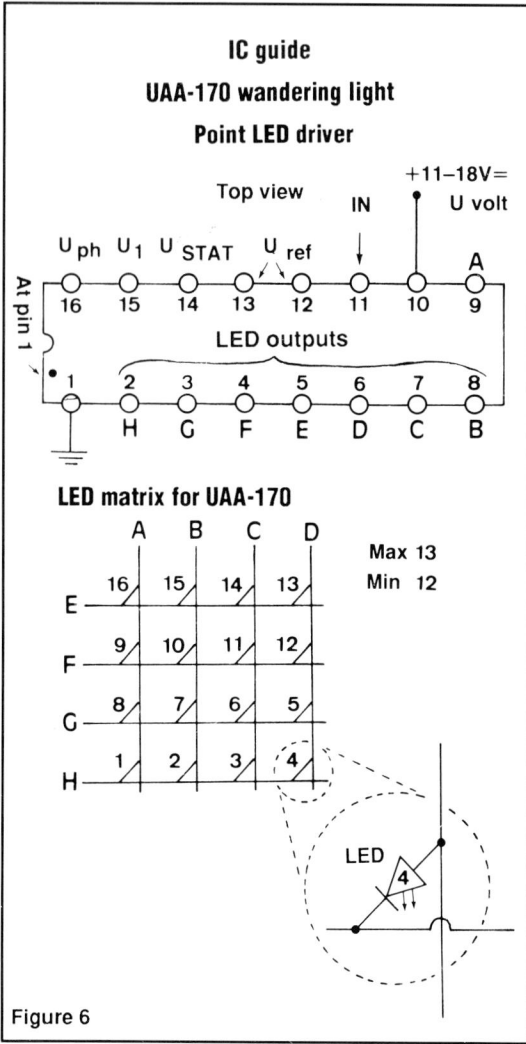

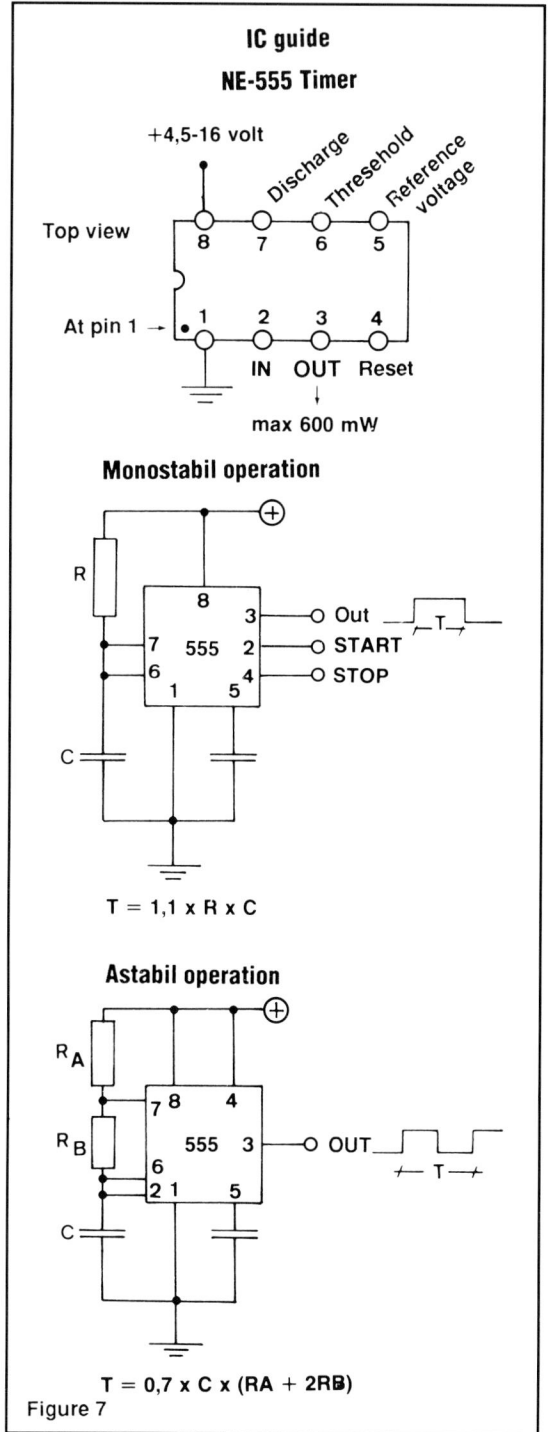

from soldering iron heat damage, use IC sockets. The sockets are soldered in place on the circuit board. The IC is inserted afterwards. Before insertation, use your multi-meter to check that plus and minus are properly connected.

CMOS ICs have many favorable characteristics. One of them is their low current drain. This can increase dramatically if you neglect to define input potential. This means that each input must be connected to something. Connect all unused inputs to either plus or minus. Outputs can be left unconnected.

IC-guide
4011 CMOS QUAD 2 input Gate

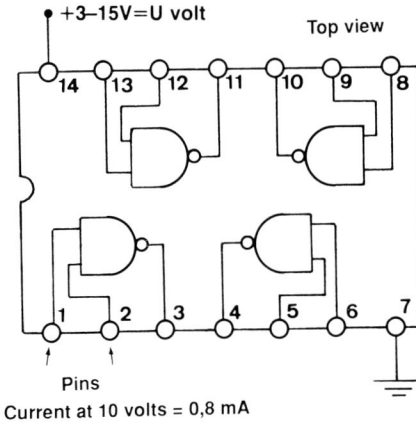

Logic table for NAND-Gate

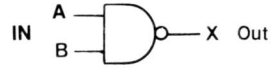

Top view

+3–15V=U volt

IN A —, B — NAND → X Out

A	B	X
0	0	1
0	1	1
1	0	1
1	1	0

0 = Ground
1 = Voltage

Pins
Current at 10 volts = 0,8 mA

Applies also to 4093 CMOS QUAD 2 input
NAND-SCHMITT trigger

Figure 8

IC guide
4017 CMOS decade counter (1 of 10 outputs is "1")

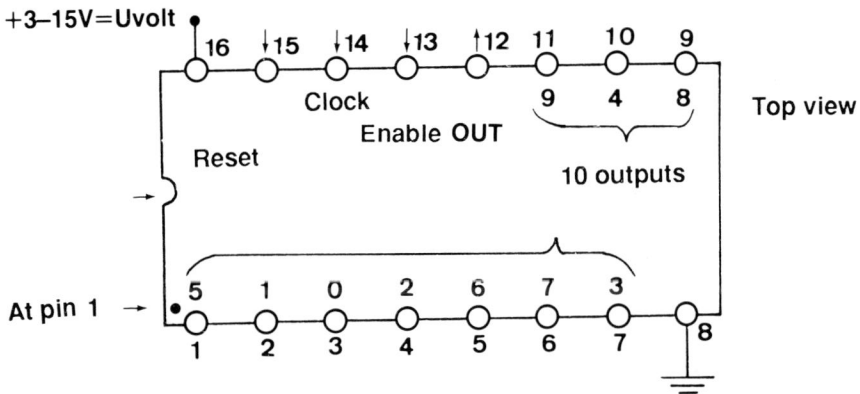

+3–15V=Uvolt

Clock
Enable OUT
Reset

9   4   8
10 outputs

Top view

At pin 1 →

5   1   0   2   6   7   3
1   2   3   4   5   6   7   8

– Current at 10 volts = 0,8 mA
– One output at a time is "1" (others "0")
– Reset and enable normally grounded
– 1 steps counts up (0 →1 →2 etc.) At ⎍ pulse at pin 14.
– Pin 12 is "1" for counting 0 - 4 and "0" for counting 5 - 9.
– Counter resets if pin 15 input is "1".
– Counter stops temporarily if pin 13 input is "1".
– 5 MHz is highest permitted frequency at 10 volts.
– Counter restarts from 0 after reaching 9.

Figure 9

93

IC-guide
4049 HEX inverter Buffer (CMOS)

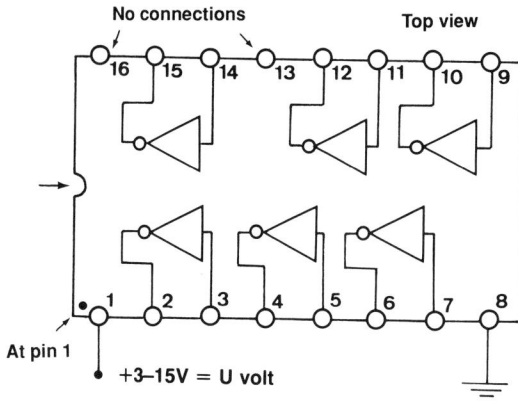

No connections   Top view

Logic table for inverted buffer

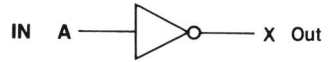

IN A   X Out

A	X
0	1
1	0

0 = Ground
1 = Voltage

At pin 1

+3–15V = U volt

Current at 10 volts = 1,6 mA

Figure 10

IC guide
40106 Hex Schmitt trigger inverter CMOS

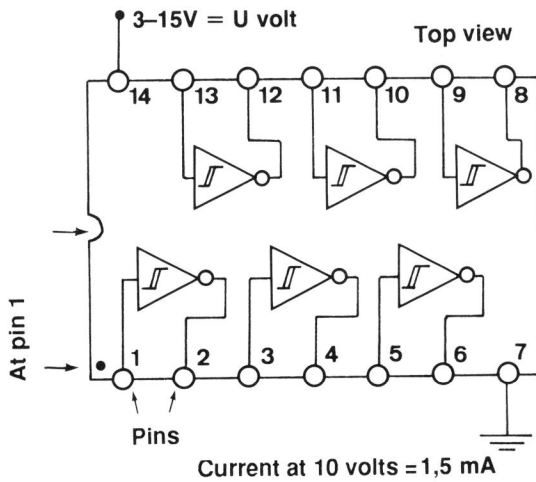

3–15V = U volt   Top view

At pin 1

Pins

Current at 10 volts = 1,5 mA

Logic table for Schmitt trigger inverter

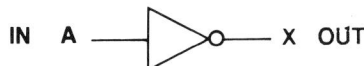

IN A   X OUT

A	X
0	I
I	0

0 = Ground
1 = Voltage

Figure 11

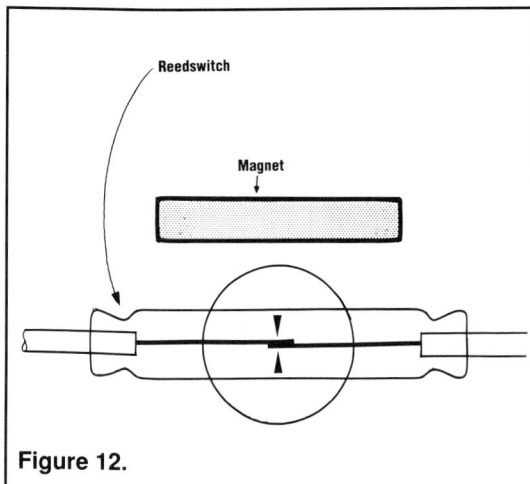
Figure 12.

A reed switch is normally open until activated by a magnet. A small magnet will need to come within 3 to 4 mm to close the contact.

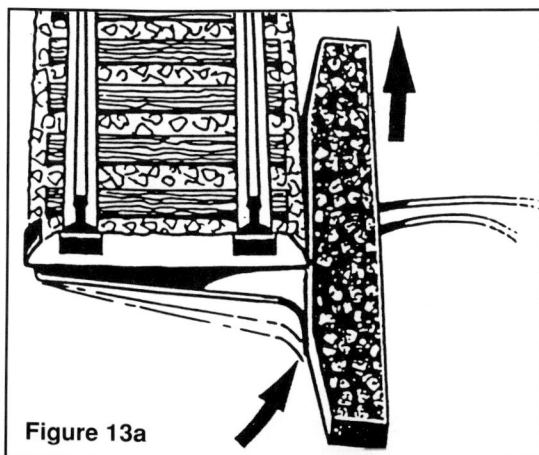
Figure 13a

This is a commercial, magnetically activated sensor. It is manufactured by Fleischmann.

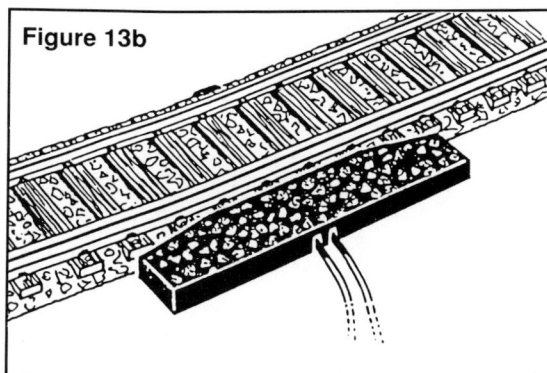
Figure 13b

REED SWITCHES (Figures 12 and 13)

They are encapsuled in clear glass tubes about a half inch long and about as thick as a match. Handle them with care. Always use needle nose pliers when bending their leads.

A reed switch has normally open contacts. The contacts are magnetically activated. A "click" is heard when the contacts close.

Reed switches are well suited to model-railroading. They are small enough for use even in the smaller scales. A magnet attached under a locomotive will momentarilly close the contacts of a track mounted reed switch. Engines without magnets pass unnoticed. In other words, you can program your trains. Programming variations are increased by varying reed switch location. They can be placed to the left, to the right and centered between the rails. A loco with a left mounted magnet will only activate one of the three switches

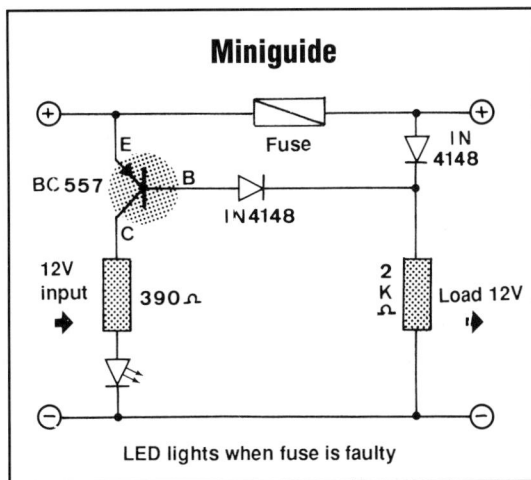

Miniguide

LED lights when fuse is faulty

Table of Contents